Painting Holiday Treasures

Inspirations from Christmas Past

Painting Holiday Treasures

Inspirations
FROM
Christmas Past

~

Pat Wakefield, MDA

NORTH LIGHT BOOKS
CINCINNATI, OHIO
www.artistsnetwork.com

Other fine North Light Books are available from your local
bookstore, art supply store or direct from the publisher.

08 07 06 05 04   5 4 3 2 1

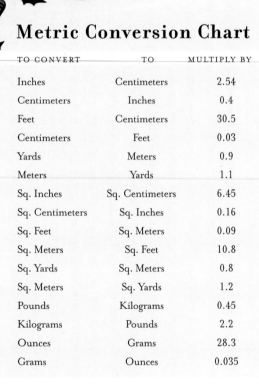

Metric Conversion Chart

TO CONVERT	TO	MULTIPLY BY
Inches	Centimeters	2.54
Centimeters	Inches	0.4
Feet	Centimeters	30.5
Centimeters	Feet	0.03
Yards	Meters	0.9
Meters	Yards	1.1
Sq. Inches	Sq. Centimeters	6.45
Sq. Centimeters	Sq. Inches	0.16
Sq. Feet	Sq. Meters	0.09
Sq. Meters	Sq. Feet	10.8
Sq. Yards	Sq. Meters	0.8
Sq. Meters	Sq. Yards	1.2
Pounds	Kilograms	0.45
Kilograms	Pounds	2.2
Ounces	Grams	28.3
Grams	Ounces	0.035

Library of Congress Cataloging-in-Publication Data

Wakefield, Pat.
   Painting holiday treasures : inspirations from Christmas past / Pat Wakefield.
   p. cm.
 Includes index.
 ISBN 1-58180-411-3
 1. Christmas decorations. 2. Painting. I. Title.

TT900.C4.W35 2004
745.594'12--dc21
                2003051419

Editor: Holly Davis
Production Coordinator: Kristen Heller
Art Director: Marissa Bowers
Layout Artist: Kathy Bergstrom
Photographers: Christine Polomsky and Al Parrish
Stylists: Kimberly Brown and Mary Barnes Clark

About the Author

For information on Pat's seminars and publications, use the following contact information:

ADDRESS:

    Pat Wakefield, MDA

    P.O. Box 3245

    Shawnee Mission, KS 66203

PHONE: 913-649-8318

E-MAIL: pat@patwakefield.com

WEB SITE: www.patwakefield.com

If you are interested in decorative painting, membership in the Society of Decorative Painters can bring you great benefits. This organization puts you in touch with more than 30,000 worldwide members through their publication, *The Decorative Painter*. Many cities have local chapters.

ADDRESS:

    The Society of Decorative Painters

    393 North McLean Boulevard

    Wichita, KS 67203-5968

PHONE: 316-269-9300

E-MAIL: sdp@decorativepainters.org

WEB SITE: www.decorativepainters.org

Pat Wakefield, MDA, is the author of twenty-eight books and thirty-nine painting packets for the decorative painter. Pat has taught classes for thirty-two years, mostly at the Cambridge House in Kansas City, Kansas, the first decorative painting shop in the country. She also teaches at shops and conventions throughout the U.S. and Canada. Her paintings and articles have been included in several international publications. She studied fine art at the University of Kansas and is a long-time member of the Society of Decorative Painters, for which she has been a judge in their certification program and has taught at several conventions. Pat received her Master Decorative Artist Certification in this society in 1975. She is versatile in her painting styles and techniques, painting with tube oils, acrylics, pastels and watercolors. Pat lives with her husband in the Kansas City area.

Table of Contents
*

Introduction

Just a few years back, most Christmas gifts were handmade. Women would sew, knit or crochet, while men made wooden items. Holiday cooking was also done at home. Sometimes candies and gingerbread boys were hung on the tree along with handmade ornaments. This put families in the spirit of the holidays and reminded them of the true meaning of Christmas. The giving of gifts you made and those special times with family were important.

Today we see people rushing around, nervously exhausting themselves with shopping, often spending much more money than they should. It's just not right! How has this happened in just over two generations? My mother talked about getting only an orange in her stocking for Christmas. Advertising has influenced our children and us into thinking we just have to have extravagant material things.

How can we change this? Perhaps if we begin, others will follow. Traditions can be revived with things like hand-painted ornaments, mantel-hung stockings and nostalgic Santas, all rekindling memories of Christmas past.

We decorative painters are fortunate that we have the ideal way of making Christmas treasures to give to others or to adorn our own homes. The items you paint from this book will be enjoyed by you, your family and your friends year after year. They may be passed down to future generations as heirlooms. Perhaps within your circle of friends and family, you'll restart the trend of making gifts and decorations. Meanwhile, you'll enjoy the creative process of making them and have the pleasure of displaying them or giving them to those you love.

Pat Wakefield, MDA

CHAPTER 1

Materials

THINGS YOU NEED TO HAVE

The supplies mentioned here are available in several places. Try small decorative painting shops, art supply shops and discount hobby stores. If a needed material is not available locally, you'll find the manufacturer's contact information under Resources on page 126.

Paints

Instructions for most of the projects in this book call for FolkArt Artists' Pigment Acrylics and FolkArt Acrylic Paints. The two Santa stockings are painted with tube oils. But there are color swatches of all the paints and paint mixtures given with each project, and you can easily substitute one type of paint for another. Just keep in mind that although the names are the same in tube oils, watercolor, gouache, casein, tube acrylics and some other brands of bottle acrylics, the painting procedures are entirely different. Also, note that you can paint with tube oils on top of acrylic basecoats but not with acrylics on top of tube oils.

FolkArt Artists' Pigment Acrylics are artist-grade paints with a creamy consistency much like tube oils. They are available in forty-six colors. The advantage of using these paints is that they are pure, standard colors with basic names used throughout the art world, but if you use these entirely, you will need to do some color mixing. FolkArt Acrylic Paints have many lovely premixed colors and save time because you can use them straight from the bottle.

Palette

For acrylics and other water-based paints, I recommend Masterson's Sta-Wet Painter's Pal palette. It comes equipped with a tight-fitting lid, palette paper and a thin sponge that slips under the palette paper to keep your paints from drying out. If a break in painting time is necessary, merely snap on the lid, and the paints will stay wet for days. If your paints should begin to dry out, merely spray them with a light mist of water. Keep the palette level to prevent water and paint from leaking under the lid.

Plastic palette boxes with lids are also available for tube oils, but I prefer a 9" x 12" (23cm x 30cm) disposable palette.

For more information about setting up your palette, see page 14 under "Setting Up Your Work Area."

Brushes

The quality of your brushes is very important. A good brushstroke cannot be made unless the brush bristles bend easily and then readily return to their original shape. Most brush companies offer several lines of brushes, and the old adage "you get what you pay for" prevails. Bristles can be either synthetic or animal hair. Good quality synthetic brushes are an acceptable economical substitute for animal hair. Always use the largest size brush that you can within the area being painted. This will eliminate excess brushstrokes and yield a softer appearance. Many brushes are designed specifically for certain techniques. Great artwork can be accomplished with a limited set of brushes as long as the selection is guided and deliberate.

Following is general information about the types of brushes used to paint the projects in this book. At the beginning of each project, you'll find a more specific brush list.

Flat

Flat brushes are used for "flat" painting such as basecoating or just filling in areas. They are also good when you want to avoid the stiff look of strokework petals painted with a round brush.

A third use of the flat is blending. Use a brush that's just damp. Start with short choppy strokes and finish with long straight strokes with a light touch. Wipe the brush often on a dry rag or paper towel. For more information about blending, see page 16.

Round

Round brushes are used to make fine lines such as stems, veins or outlining. They are also used for painting dots or comma-shaped strokes. For line work, thin the paint to an ink-like consistency. For strokework, thin the paint to the fluidity of nail polish. Load your brush until all hairs are wet, but avoid filling it to the ferrule (metal part).

Liner

Liner brushes are long, round, thin and pointed. Use them to make very fine lines.

Pat Wakefield's Deer Foot by Bette Byrd: *This brush creates the textural effect of fuzzy animal fur or foliage.*

Scroller

The scroller is also used for fine lines, but it is fuller than the liner and holds more paint.

Stencil

A stencil brush can be used to stipple paint with or without a stencil.

Fan

This brush has a fan shape with hairs which separate. Use of this brush will produce a streaked effect good for painting grass or animal fur. The fan is also a great blender to soften, but not eliminate, brush marks.

Deerfoot

This brush has a round ferrule and bristles cut on an angle, giving them the shape of a deer's foot. You can use the deerfoot to stipple fuzzy animal fur or foliage. Because I made the deerfoot popular, Bette Byrd Brushes calls theirs "Pat Wakefield's Deer Foot." This stiff brush should be loaded with dry paint and pounced onto the surface. For more information on using the deerfoot, see pages 95-96.

Whisk, Comb, Rake

Use a whisk, comb, or rake brush to paint grass, hair or animal fur. These brushes' bristles are spread and of varying length, giving a streaked effect.

Flat Sponge

This sponge on a stick handle is used for basecoating large areas. It is also called a foam brush.

Other Supplies

You'll need a few additional supplies besides paint, a palette and brushes. These commonly used items are used for projects in this book.

- WOOD SEALER: to seal wood before painting.
- SANDPAPER, 400-GRIT: used to sand wood pieces.
- TACK CLOTH: for cleaning off sanding dust.
- SCISSORS: for cutting paper for patterns.
- TRACING PAPER: to trace patterns for transfer.
- BLACK AND WHITE TRANSFER PAPER: for transferring patterns to pieces to be painted.
- STYLUS: to trace patterns onto the painting surface. A pen may be used instead.
- KNEADED ERASER: to remove excess graphite from pattern tracings.
- COMPASS: to draw circles. You may substitute mixing bowls for large circles or a circle template for small circles.
- RULER: for a variety of measuring tasks.

When painting on wood, start by covering the surface with wood sealer. When painting with acrylics, no matter what the surface, finish with acrylic sealer.

- PALETTE KNIFE: a tool for mixing paint on your palette.
- FOLKART BLENDING GEL: for mixing with acrylic paints to add transparency or to moisten surfaces prior to painting. This medium increases the open time of acrylic paint while maintaining paint thickness. Using Blending Gel allows for blending colors, shading or highlighting.
- COBALT SICCATIVE DRIER: to speed drying of tube oils
- WINSOR & NEWTON BLENDING & GLAZING MEDIUM: a gel mixture to use with tube oil paints.
- SCOTCH PLASTIC TAPE 471 BLUE: for masking curves. This stretchable tape is available at auto paint stores.
- SCOTCH MAGIC TAPE: for masking straight lines.
- PAPER TOWELS: for wiping your brush and for cleanup.
- BRUSH BASIN: to rinse brushes.
- SPRAY BOTTLE: to dampen your palette as the paint dries.
- SMALL PLASTIC CONTAINERS WITH TIGHT-FITTING LIDS: to save paint mixtures. A 35mm film can works well.
- HAIR DRYER: to speed drying time of mediums and paints.
- BRUSH PLUS BRUSH CLEANER FROM PLAID: to thoroughly clean brushes.
- FOLKART CLEARCOTE ACRYLIC SEALER: to use as a finishing coat on wood pieces or on canvas painted with acrylic paints.
- GRUMBACHER PICTURE VARNISH: to use as a finishing coat over tube oil paints.

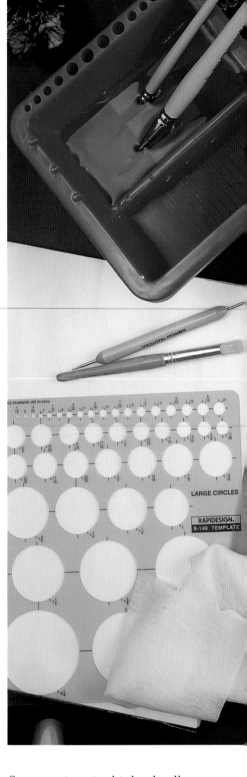

Some projects in this book call for specialized supplies. Be sure you consult the project materials list before starting your work.

Painting Surfaces

Papier-mâché, wood, porcelain and fabric painting surfaces are used in this
book. However, don't feel limited by these. You can find other suitable
items at craft stores or wood shops in your area. A photocopy machine will
enlarge or reduce a pattern to accommodate a different surface.

CHAPTER 2

Basics

THINGS YOU NEED TO KNOW

Preparing the Surface

If you are using a wood surface, seal the wood with wood sealer. Wait one hour and then sand the surface with 400-grit sandpaper along the grain of the wood. Wipe off the sanding dust with a tack cloth. Basecoat the surface, letting it dry for several hours before transferring the pattern.

If you are using a porcelain surface, you only need to sand lightly. Some porcelain is rather absorbent, so spray the surface with a light coat of FolkArt Acrylic Sealer.

If you are using a canvas surface, such as the canvas-covered address book on pages 46-55, just apply a basecoat of acrylic paint. If you want to stiffen the fabric, such as with the Santa stockings on pages 100-125, apply two coats of FolkArt Textile Medium before basecoating.

Transferring The Pattern

Tape the transfer paper and the pattern to the painting surface. Be sure the transfer paper is shiny side down and under the pattern. Trace over the pattern lines with a pen or stylus. If you place a sheet of waxed paper on top of the pattern, the impressions will show you which lines you've traced. (See step 9, page 106.) If the traced pattern lines are quite heavy, remove some of the tracing with a kneaded eraser.

Setting Up Your Work Area

Place your prepared project surface in front of you on a table. If you're right-handed, your palette should be to the right of the project. If left-handed, to the left.

For acrylics I recommend Masterson's Sta-Wet Painter's Pal palette. Prepare it by dipping the palette sponge into water and then wringing it to remove the excess.

HINT

Use a loose-leaf notebook filled with plastic page covers to keep track of project reference material, such as copies of the pattern and instructions, paint swatches of color changes and photos of your finished piece. This system is easy to maintain and saves you the exasperation of searching through piles of papers.

Soak the palette paper in water for a few minutes and place this on top of the palette sponge.

For tube oils I prefer a 9" x 12" (23cm x 30cm) disposable palette. For both acrylics and tube oils, you will then need to lay out a paper towel, your brushes and a palette knife. For acrylics you will also need a water basin; for tube oils, a dish of paint thinner.

If you're painting with acrylics, squeeze out a fifty-cent-coin size puddle of each color needed along one side of your palette. Always add extra white.

If you're painting with oils, squeeze out only a capful of each color. Oils require smaller amounts than acrylics. You can always squeeze more out, but you can't return the paint to the tube.

Arrange the colors in an order that makes sense to you. To help you become familiar with color names, write them on the palette next to each puddle.

Loading the Brush

Dip your brush in water for acrylics or in paint thinner for oils and dry it on a paper towel before picking up paint. If the paint is stiff, dip the corner of the brush in water or Blending Gel (for acrylics) or paint thinner (for oils) and then into the paint. Work the paint and medium together on your palette with your brush.

Preparing Paint Mixtures

Paint seems to spread while mixing and can take up a lot of space. For this reason, you may want to mix your paints on a separate sheet of palette paper and then transfer them to your painting palette. In this book, paint-mix formulas are given with each set of project instructions. On the palette paper beside each mixture, write the mix number used in the instructions.

With both acrylics and oils, it's best to mix more paint than you think you'll need. Remixing exact color matches is difficult, and it's frustrating to run out in the middle of the painting. Using the Painter's Pal palette described on page 10 is one way to keep acrylics wet during painting breaks. To preserve a tube

HINT

Be cautious with the materials you're using. The pigment that gives paint its color is toxic, and breathing the pigment is the most hazardous way of ingesting it. Work in a well-ventilated room, wash your hands often and do not smoke or eat while painting.

CREATING A PAINT MIX

1. Place all colors included in the mix on a separate sheet of palette paper. With a palette knife, scrape up a small amount of the second color in the mix and press it into the first.

2. Scrape and press the combined paints again and again until the colors are mixed. Repeat the process with additional mix colors, if used.

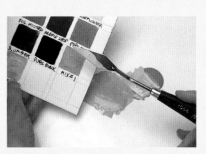

3. Check to see if your mix matches the desired color. Adjust if necessary, remembering that acrylics will appear darker when dry.

After creating all your mixes, transfer them to the palette sheet you will use while painting.

oil palette, add a drop of Winsor & Newton Blending and Glazing Medium to each pile of paint and cover the palette with plastic wrap. Small plastic containers with tight lids, such as those used for 35mm film, also work well for storing paints.

To create a paint mix, place on your palette each color included. Start with the first color listed because these formulas start with the predominant color. With your palette knife, pick up a small amount of the next color from the formula and press it into the first color. Scrape up the pile and press it together again and again until the colors are thoroughly mixed. Wipe your palette knife on a paper towel.

Adjust colors to match the color swatch in the project instructions. Remember that acrylic paints appear darker when dry than when wet, so it's best to let your paint sample dry to be sure of the match. You will not have this problem with tube oils.

When only a small amount of paint mix is needed, you can brush-mix colors. To do this, merely dip into one color and then into the next. Stroke the brush on the palette to mix the colors in the brush. Then apply your mix to the painting.

Blending

Blending is a brush technique that fuses shading colors to create a gradual transition from light to dark. This technique differs for acrylics and tube oils.

Acrylics

1. Basecoat the area to be blended with several coats of your chosen color (usually the medium value) until the area is well covered. Let each coat dry thoroughly or the undercoat will lift from the surface.
2. To add a shading (darker) color, first apply a coat of FolkArt Blending Gel, which will retard the drying time.
3. While the area is wet, recoat it with the basecoat color thinned with Blending Gel and applied very lean. Immediately add a second color, also lean, and blend the two with a soft flat brush. This same process is used for adding highlighting

(lighter) colors. In either case, the procedure may take several coats.
4. Another technique is to first basecoat each area thoroughly and then float on the shading or highlighting color. To do this, wait until the basecoat is dry. Load a flat brush with Blending Gel, and then load the shading or highlighting color on just one side of the brush. Apply this paint to the basecoated area.

Tube Oils

1. Basecoat a section of the painting with a medium-value paint color, adding only enough Winsor & Newton Blending & Glazing Medium to cause the paint to spread easily yet still be opaque. Use a soft flat brush, the largest size you can handle for the project.
2. Add shading either over the basecoat or beside the basecoat. With a soft, dry flat brush, blend the two colors together, starting with a slip-slap stroke and finishing with a smooth, light blending stroke. Wipe the brush often on a rag or paper towel to eliminate excess paint. Repeat for highlight colors.
3. With a soft, dry mop brush, blend very lightly to remove any brushstrokes.

Cleaning the Brush

Your brush can be cleaned between colors with water for acrylics or with paint thinner for oils; however, this is necessary only when making a drastic change, such as from white to black. Otherwise, merely wipe your brush on a paper towel before switching to the next color. Do treat your brushes with care and don't scrub them on the paper towel.

Clean brushes thoroughly after each painting session. When painting with acrylics, rinse the brushes in your water basin; when painting with tube oils, rinse brushes in paint thinner. Then clean with Brush Plus followed by soap and cool water. Rinse again in clear water. Shape the brushes flat or pointed and place them in a location where the hairs are not touching anything. Allow them to dry.

If a brush becomes unruly, run the clean brush over a bar of mild soap. Let the soap dry to shape the brush. Rinse the brush before your next painting session.

Drying and Finishing

Acrylic paints dry rapidly. To further speed the drying process, use a hair dryer. When the painting is finished, you will want to add a finishing coat to protect your project and to add richness to the color. For wood pieces, spray on two coats of FolkArt Clearcote Acrylic Sealer. This sealer is also good for fabric and porcelain.

To speed the drying time of tube oils, add small drops of cobalt siccative drier to your paints on the palette. Be especially careful with this product, as it is highly toxic. Add Grumbacher Picture Varnish as the final coat.

PAINTER'S CHECKLIST

As important as assembling proper materials and learning the basics of painting are, they're not the only considerations. Before you begin any project, be sure you've thought it through. The checklist below covers everything from putting yourself in the right frame of mind to organizing your workplace.

✔ Choose a project that interests you. Encourage yourself to give a seemingly difficult project a try. Remember that your work doesn't have to resemble the original but can be your own interpretation.

✔ If this project is to be a Christmas gift, ask yourself if you will have time to complete it. If not, ask yourself if that matters.

✔ If you need to order a painting surface, do so.

✔ If you choose a painting surface different from that in the book, determine whether you need to change the pattern size. Remember that with a photocopy machine, you can enlarge or reduce the pattern to fit your need.

✔ Make sure you have all the materials listed at the beginning of the project, such as paint colors, correct brush types and sizes, painting gel, and so on.

✔ Read through chapter one on supplies (pages 10-13) to see whether additional items would be helpful.

✔ Determine a time to paint when interruptions will be minimal.

✔ Find a place where you can leave your work out for several days if necessary.

✔ Lay out all your supplies on a table where you will be working.

✔ Organize your work area, keeping clutter to a minimum. Order promotes better painting.

✔ Read through the instructions to get an overall idea of what you'll be doing.

You are now ready to begin.

MATERIALS

✦ **Surface**
Papier-mâché star-shaped box, 11" x 11" (28cm x 28cm) lid, from Viking Woodcrafts. (See Resources on page 126.)

✦ **Bette Byrd Brushes**
- no. 2 flat
- no. 4 flat
- no. 6 flat
- no. 20 flat
- no. 1 liner

✦ **Other**
- Plaid stencil brush

✦ **Additional Supplies**
- hair dryer
- white transfer paper
- pen or stylus
- Scotch Plastic Tape 471 Blue, ⅛" (3mm) and ¼" (6mm)
- FolkArt Blending Gel
- FolkArt Clearcote Acrylic Sealer

Poinsettia Box

This would be a special gift box for a Christmas present. The recipient could then have many opportunities to display it during the holidays as a centerpiece or on an end table with greenery around it. The striping is uncomplicated and adds a distinctive effect.

Papier-mâché boxes like this one are inexpensive and lightweight, yet sturdy and easy to work with. These boxes are available in several sizes or as a nested set.

Paint: FolkArt Acrylics

930 PRIMROSE

924 THICKET

958 CHRISTMAS RED

646 ASPEN GREEN

922 BAYBERRY

901 WICKER WHITE

Paint: FolkArt Metallics

676 INCA GOLD

577 SAHARA GOLD

Paint: FolkArt Artists' Pigment

918 YELLOW LIGHT

628 PURE ORANGE

629 RED LIGHT

758 ALIZARIN CRIMSON

463 DIOXAZINE PURPLE

479 PURE BLACK

PATTERN

This pattern may be hand-traced or photocopied for personal use only. Enlarge at 178% to bring up to full size.

SURFACE PREPARATION

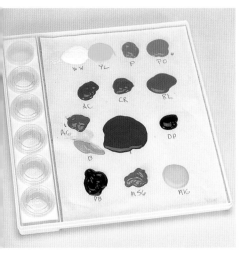

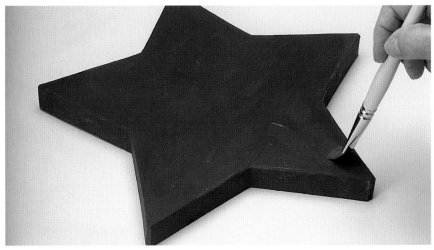

1. Arrange the paints on the palette in color families. Mark with pen the initials of each color to help you identify them by name.

2. Paint the lid of the box with several coats of Thicket, using the no. 20 flat. Use a hair dryer to speed the drying of each coat.

3. Cut out the pattern to fit the shape of the box. Tape two edges of the pattern to the box lid, and then slip the transfer paper between the pattern and the lid. Trace the pattern with a pen or stylus, lifting the paper periodically to check what you've traced.

4. Paint the sides of the box bottom with several coats of Primrose, using the no. 20 flat. Add several coats of Christmas Red.

HINT

Christmas Red is not a good covering color and, for this reason, does not work well as a basecoat. By using Primrose first, the Christmas Red goes on smoothly.

BOX STRIPES

5. Use ¼" (6mm) Scotch Plastic Tape to mask off vertical spaces around the sides of the box. These spaces may be measured or "eyeballed."

6. After placing tape all around the box, paint two or three lightly applied coats between the taped edges with Sahara Gold on a no. 4 flat. This is how the paint looks after one coat.

7. Peel off the tape while the paint is wet so the tape will be less likely to tear the basecoat. If any basecoat comes off, just reapply the Primrose and Christmas Red as needed.

LID STIPPLING AND STRIPE

8. Dip a small dry stencil brush into Inca Gold and dab it on a paper towel so you have a small amount of paint.

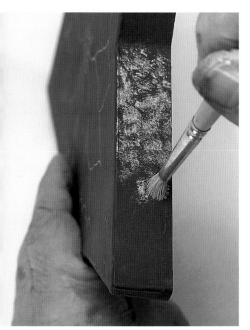

9. Stipple the border edge.

10. Place ⅛" (3mm) Scotch Plastic Tape around the lid's bottom edge. Place another strip about ¼" (6mm) above the first strip. You can probably eyeball the placement of the tape without measuring. Paint two coats of Inca Gold between the tape lines, using a no. 4 flat. Peel off the tape.

GREEN LEAVES

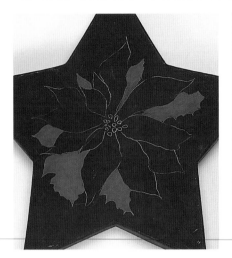

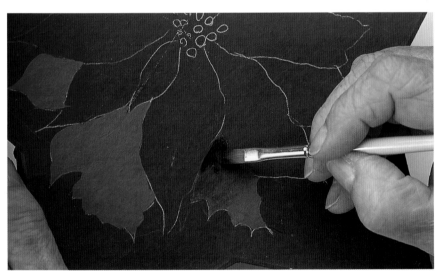

11. Basecoat the green leaves with Aspen Green and a no. 6 flat. Use this photo to help you distinguish between the green leaves and the red leaves (bracts), which you will paint later.

12. With a no. 6 flat, pick up a tiny bit of Blending Gel and then Thicket. Shade where the leaves overlap, blending softly into the Aspen Green. Blending is easier when both colors are wet, so you may want to paint one leaf at a time.

13. Add Pure Black to leaves with the darkest areas and blend. The photo with step 15 shows the placement of all three darker areas.

14. Lighten the leaf points with Bayberry and a no. 6 flat, blending into the darker greens. You may need several coats. The photo with step 15 shows the placement of these lighter areas.

15. This shows the shading and highlighting of all the green leaves.

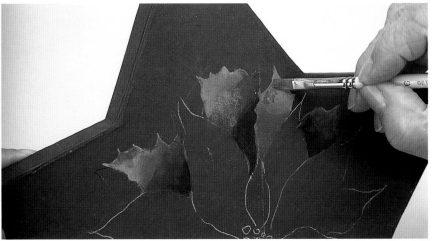

16. Tint a few of the leaves with Christmas Red and a no. 6 flat.

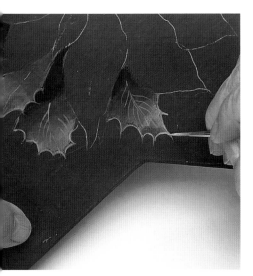

17. Paint the veins using the no. 1 liner. For the light veins, brush-mix a little Wicker White + Bayberry, thinned with water to an ink-like consistency. Outline these leaves in the same color.

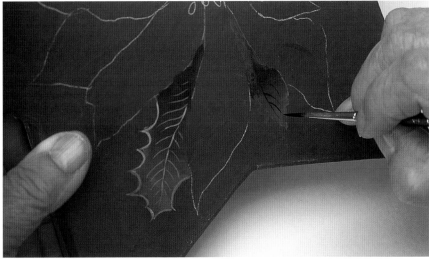

18. Paint the dark veins with a no. 1 liner and Pure Black.

RED BRACTS

19. Basecoat the red bracts in Primrose with a no. 6 flat. For complete coverage, apply three coats, but avoid covering the pattern lines. This photo shows the coverage after two coats.

20. Paint the bracts again with Red Light and a no. 6 flat.

21. Use the no. 6 flat and work on one bract at a time, keeping the paint moist. Repaint the bract with Red Light and then shade the dark parts with Alizarin Crimson mixed with a very small amount of Dioxazine Purple. Paint right over the center flower heads. This shading may take several coats. Don't worry if the shading colors don't seem to blend with the previous colors.

22. Mix Christmas Red with Blending Gel on a no. 6 flat. Keeping the color transparent, apply it to the bract and blend until smooth. This procedure, called glazing, evens out the colors.

23. Highlight one bract at a time. First paint the light parts of the bract with Red Light on the no. 6 flat.

24. Lighten further with Pure Orange.

25. The lightest bracts are painted with Pure Orange + a small amount of Wicker White. Repeat steps 23 through 25 on all the highlighted bracts.

26. Paint the veins with Wicker White + a small amount of Pure Orange on the no. 1 liner. Thin with water to an ink-like consistency.

27. A few dark veins are painted with Alizarin Crimson thinned with water and the no. 1 liner.

YELLOW FLOWERS

28. Redraw the flower heads with white transfer paper or sketch them in white paint.

29. Paint the flower heads with Aspen Green on a no. 2 flat. Darken with Thicket plus a touch of Pure Black.

30. Lighten the flower heads with Bayberry on the no. 2 flat.

31. Add spots of Pure Orange, using the no. 2 flat.

32. Add spots of Yellow Light into the centers with the no. 2 flat.

COMPLETED POINSETTIA BOX

33. Spray on two coats of FolkArt
Clearcote Acrylic Sealer, letting it dry
between coats.

MATERIALS

✦ **Surface**
   Porcelain ornaments,
   5½" (14cm) from tip
   to tip, from Viking
   Woodcrafts.
   (See Resources on page 126.)

✦ **Bette Byrd Brushes**
   · no. 1 flat (P)
   · no. 2 flat (W&C, H, W)
   · no. 4 flat (W&C, H, W, P)
   · no. 1 round (W&C, H)
   · no. 1 liner (W&C, H, W, P)
   · no. 1 scroller (P)

✦ **Additional Supplies**
   · 400-grit sandpaper
   · tack cloth
   · gold leaf adhesive size
     (apply with old no. 4 flat)
   · gold leaf
   · Burnt Umber tube oil
   · Winsor & Newton
     Blending & Glazing Medium
   · paper towel
   · black transfer paper
     and stylus
   · FolkArt Blending Gel
   · FolkArt Clearcote
     Acrylic Sealer

Ornament Materials Key

W&C - Used on
         "Warm and Cozy"

H - Used on "Holly"

W - Used on "Wreath"

P - Used on "Pine Trees"

Four Porcelain Ornaments

Every Christmas I paint one of these porcelain ornaments for each of my seven grandchildren, including the grandchild's name and the date on the back. The ornaments will be lifetime heirlooms, so I keep the designs traditional. The gold leaf trim adds a richness, and the fragility of the porcelain seems to make them just a little more special. Porcelain requires little preparation other than a light sanding, so you are ready to paint in minutes.

Paint: FolkArt Acrylics

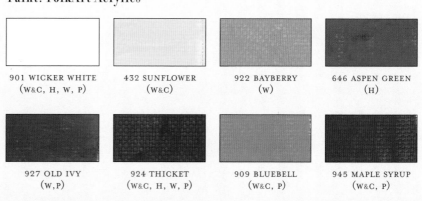

| 901 WICKER WHITE (W&C, H, W, P) | 432 SUNFLOWER (W&C) | 922 BAYBERRY (W) | 646 ASPEN GREEN (H) |

| 927 OLD IVY (W, P) | 924 THICKET (W&C, H, W, P) | 909 BLUEBELL (W&C, P) | 945 MAPLE SYRUP (W&C, P) |

Paint: FolkArt Artists' Pigment

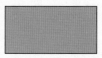

| 479 PURE BLACK (H) | 758 ALIZARIN CRIMSON (H, W) | 629 RED LIGHT (W&C, H, W) | 628 PURE ORANGE (W&C, H, W) |

PATTERNS

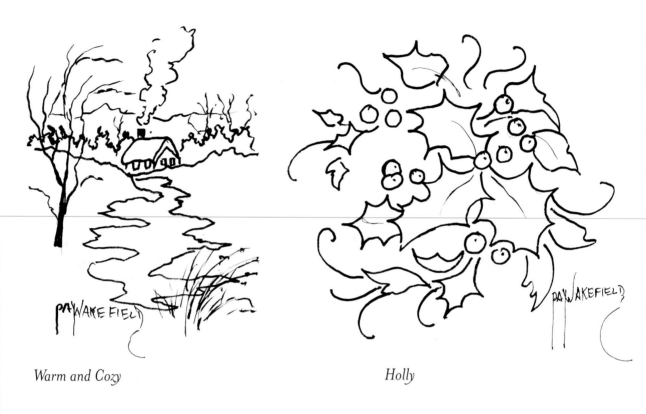

Warm and Cozy

Holly

Wreath

Pine Trees

These patterns may be hand-traced or photocopied for personal use only. These patterns are at full size.

SURFACE PREPARATION & LEAFING

1. Sand the ornament with 400-grit sandpaper until smooth. Remove the dust with a tack cloth. Paint the points on the ornament using Red Light on a no. 4 flat.

2. Let dry and apply a coat of gold leaf adhesive size to the points with a no. 4 flat. Use an old brush and wash it immediately because the sizing is difficult to remove when the brush is dry. Wait until the sizing is clear and just tacky—about 15 minutes. Cut or tear pieces of gold leaf into 1-inch (2.5cm) squares and lay them one at a time onto the tacky sizing. Overlap the pieces, brushing with a soft dry no. 4 flat brush and allowing some cracks of Red Light to show through.

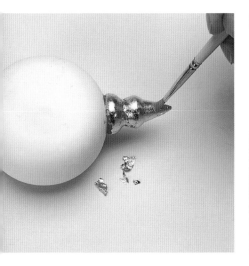

HINT

Mixing Blending & Glazing Medium with Burnt Umber tube oil creates a glaze you can apply over gold leaf to dull it slightly.

3. After applying the gold leaf, continue brushing to remove all the small pieces. Wait 24 hours and brush again to give a burnished appearance.

4. Mix a small amount of Burnt Umber tube oil with a few drops of Winsor & Newton Blending & Glazing Medium. Apply a coat to the gold leaf and wipe with a soft rag or paper towel to the desired shade. This should only soften the glare of the gold leaf a bit. Let dry.

WARM AND COZY

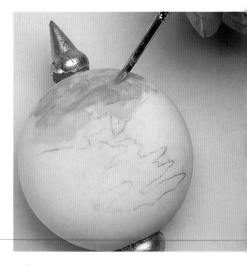

5. Transfer the pattern onto the ornament as described on page 14. Leave off the stick trees.

6. Use acrylic Blending Gel with all the paints on this project to aid blendability. Paint the sky with Sunflower, using a no. 2 flat brush.

7. Add Bluebell over the Sunflower on the upper sky. Blend slightly.

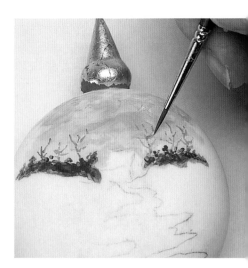

8. Just above the house, add a touch of Pure Orange and blend.

9. Dab on the background trees with Thicket on a no. 2 flat. Along the top edge of the trees, apply spots of the same color with a no. 1 round.

10. Using Maple Syrup and a no. 1 liner brush, freehand the fine-line stick trees in the far background.

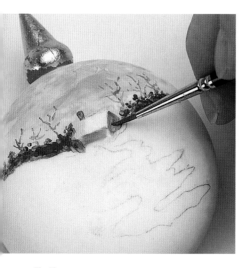

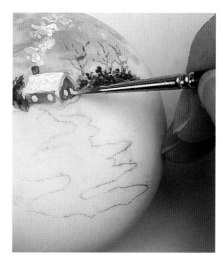

11. Paint the house using a no. 1 liner brush with Pure Orange. Darken with Maple Syrup, making the right end darkest. Also paint the chimney with Maple Syrup.

12. Paint the smoke coming from the chimney using Wicker White on a no. 1 liner. Also paint the roof with Wicker White, shading the right end with Bluebell.

13. Paint the windows with Sunflower on the no. 1 liner.

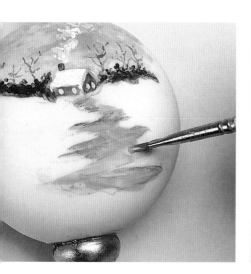

14. Paint the stream with a no. 2 flat, using Bluebell + Sunflower along with Blending Gel. Streak the paint horizontally. Darken the shoreline using Maple Syrup.

15. Paint the snow with Wicker White on a no. 2 flat. Add shading with Bluebell.

16. Paint the large tree and the Weeds with Maple Syrup + Thicket on a no. 1 liner.

When the ornament is dry, spray it with just a mist of FolkArt Clearcote Acrylic Sealer.

Completed ornament is on page 38.

HOLLY

1. Prepare the ornament as described on page 33. Brush on Thicket in the area where the design is to be painted, using the no. 2 flat brush. Mix a little Blending Gel with the paint. Soften the edge of this area by wiping with a soft paper towel and blending with the dry brush. This will give a clouded effect. Two coats may be needed.

Transfer the pattern to the ornament as described on page 14.

2. Paint the dark leaves with the no. 2 flat using Thicket. Paint the lighter leaves with Aspen Green.

3. Lighten one side of these light leaves with the addition of Wicker White.

Paint the veins and outlining on the light leaves with Wicker White. Use the no. 1 liner brush.

4. Paint the vines with Thicket on the no. 1 liner brush. Then paint the berries with a no. 1 round. Start with Red Light.

5. Add Alizarin Crimson to darken. Add Pure Orange to lighten.

6. Add a Pure Black dot. Add a Wicker White dot as a highlight.

When the ornament is dry, spray it with just a mist of FolkArt Clearcote Acrylic Sealer.

Completed ornament is on page 38.

WREATH

1. Prepare the ornament as described on page 33. You may wish to paint this design freehand. If not, transfer the pattern as described on page 14. With Thicket on the no. 1 liner brush, start making pine branches and needles. Place these around the inner and outer edges of the wreath.

2. Throughout the central part of the wreath, add a few strokes, using Old Ivy. Then paint the light branches and needles, some with Bayberry and some with Bayberry + Wicker White.

3. Add a few dots of Thicket. With the no. 1 liner, paint the berries with Red Light, Alizarin Crimson and Pure Orange.

Paint the bow with Red Light, using the no. 2 flat. Darken with Alizarin Crimson and lighten with Pure Orange.

When the ornament is dry, spray it with just a mist of FolkArt Clearcote Acrylic Sealer.

Completed ornament is on page 39.

PINE TREES

1. Prepare the ornament as described on page 33. Transfer the pattern as described on page 14. Paint the sky with a no. 1 flat using Bluebell + a little Wicker White.

Paint the mountains with Wicker White.

2. Paint the background trees using Old Ivy on a no. 1 liner brush. Paint the foreground trees with Thicket on a no. 1 liner brush. Add snow on the branches with Wicker White.

3. Water is Bluebell and Bluebell + Maple Syrup. Snow and ice are Wicker White. Streak on horizontally with a no. 1 flat. Add weeds with a no. 1 scroller and Maple Syrup + Thicket. When the ornament is dry, spray on a mist of FolkArt Clearcote Acrylic Sealer. Completed ornament is on page 39.

COMPLETED ORNAMENTS

Warm and Cozy

Holly

Wreath

Pine Trees

MATERIALS

✦ **Surface**
Punched-tin round container with 13½" (34cm) diameter wooden lid from Viking Woodcrafts. (See Resources on page 126.)

✦ **Bette Byrd Brushes**
- no. 2 flat
- no. 4 flat
- no. 20 flat
- no. 1 round
- no. 1 liner

✦ **Other**
- 1-inch (25mm) flat sponge brush

✦ **Additional Supplies**
- 400-grit sandpaper
- tack cloth
- paper towels
- white transfer paper and stylus
- FolkArt Clearcote Acrylic Sealer

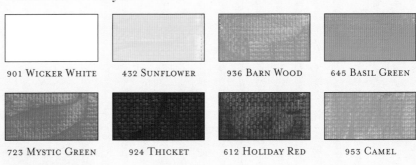

Boxwood and Fruit Wreath Tin

Boxwood foliage is an attractive Christmas greenery and makes a refreshing change from the more common pine wreath. This evergreen shrub, which can grow into a tree if not pruned, has very hard wood used for carving.

Originating in England, boxwood is found mostly in the eastern part of the United States, including Mount Vernon. Dried fruit, such as that on my wreath, has long-established decorative use and goes well with the punched-tin container so reminiscent of an earlier American era.

Paint: FolkArt Acrylics

901 WICKER WHITE	432 SUNFLOWER	936 BARN WOOD	645 BASIL GREEN
723 MYSTIC GREEN	924 THICKET	612 HOLIDAY RED	953 CAMEL
959 ENGLISH MUSTARD			

Paint: FolkArt Acrylics & Artists' Pigment

MIX 1: PURE ORANGE + MYSTIC GREEN (1:1)

MIX 2: WICKER WHITE + PURE ORANGE (2:1)

Paint: FolkArt Artists' Pigment

628 PURE ORANGE   462 BURNT UMBER   629 RED LIGHT

PATTERN AND BACKGROUND

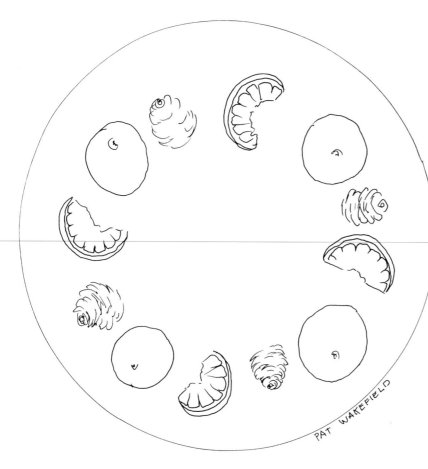

This pattern may be hand-traced or photocopied for personal use only.
Enlarge at 200%. Then enlarge again at 104% to bring up to full size.

1. Using a 1-inch (25mm) flat sponge brush, paint the lid front, back and edges with one coat of Barn Wood thinned with water to an ink-like consistency. Paint with the grain of the wood running vertically

2. Let the paint dry and then sand the lid with 400-grit sandpaper until smooth. Wipe clean with a tack cloth.

3. Paint the lid a second time in thinned Barn Wood, using the no. 20 flat. (See the left side of Illustration 1.) Paint the entire lid front and curved edge with water-thinned Thicket. Blend, leaving the paint somewhat streaked with the grain, as you see the right side of Illustration 1.

4. Lighten the center area of the lid front with Sunflower and Basil Green, as shown in Illustration 1.

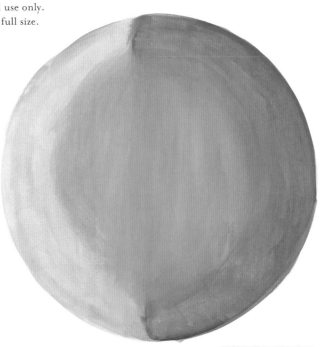

ILLUSTRATION 1

WREATH

ILLUSTRATION 2

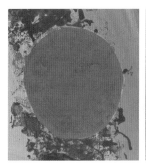

7. Basecoat the apples with two coats of Mix 2 on a no. 4 flat brush.

8. Paint the apples again with two coats of Red Light. Shade around the outer edge with Holiday Red.

9. Paint the orange sections with Mix 1 on a no. 2 flat.

10. Streak these sections using a no. 1 round and Holiday Red, then Pure Orange and then Mix 2. Outline the sections with a no. 1 liner and Wicker White. Shade the lower part of these sections with a little Basil Green.

5. Use paper towels to basecoat the wreath in Thicket. First wad the towel and dip it into the paint. Then dab this towel on a dry paper towel to remove some paint. Finally, dab the paint-dipped towel onto the wood. Keep this area at about 1½" (4cm) width—narrow enough so that leaves can be painted outside the edges.

6. Transfer the pattern of the apples and oranges as you see at the bottom of Illustration 2. (Pattern transfer instructions are on page 14.) The leaves are best painted freehand.

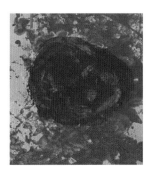

11. Paint an oval pine cone shape with Burnt Umber on a no. 4 flat.

12. With a no. 1 round, lay curved strokes across the oval with English Mustard. Overlap these with strokes of Camel.

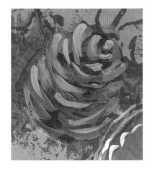

WREATH, CONTINUED

ILLUSTRATION 3

15. Paint the orange skin with a no. 1 liner and Pure Orange. Shade the lower part of the skin area with Thicket.

16. The leaves and stems are best painted freehand. Start with the darkest values and then work into the medium and lightest values, always using a no. 1 round brush. Press your strokes from the leaf base and lift to the point.

Paint the darkest leaves using Thicket. Paint the second layer, which will overlap some of the first layer, using Mystic Green. The third layer is Basil Green. For the very lightest leaves, add a little Wicker White to some Basil Green.

17. Paint the berries with a no. 1 round, starting with Holiday Red. Add spots of Pure Orange, followed with a more precise Wicker White highlight spot.

18. Spray the lid with two coats of FolkArt Clearcote Acrylic Sealer, letting it dry between coats.

13. Shade the apple edges with Thicket on a no. 4 flat.

14. Use Illustration 3 and the photos on page 45 to help you place the rest of the apple colors. With a no. 1 round, start painting the apple "dimple" with a spot of Basil Green. Pull your strokes up from the dimple, following the curve. Add a little Thicket next to the Basil Green to resemble a stem. Add a dot of Wicker White. Paint the stem highlight with Holiday Red, pulling strokes up from the dimple and following the curve. In the same manner, paint some apple highlights with Mix 2 on a no. 2 flat. Add several Wicker White highlights.

COMPLETED WREATH TIN

Top View

Side View

MATERIALS

✦ **Surface**
Canvas-covered address book, 6" x 9" (15cm x 23cm), from Viking Woodcrafts. (See Resources on page 126.)

✦ **Bette Byrd Brushes**
- no. 2 flat
- no. 4 flat
- no. 20 flat
- no. 1 round
- no. 1 liner

✦ **Additional Supplies**
- ¼" (6mm) Scotch Plastic Tape 471 Blue
- black transfer paper and stylus
- FolkArt Blending Gel
- dry brush (for softening colors)
- paper towels (optional)
- FolkArt Clearcote Acrylic Sealer

Winter Scene Address Book

This scene lends itself to a variety of surfaces, such as a box or a canvas to be framed. As an address book, you might choose to use it for your Christmas card list. The theme need not be used strictly for Christmas, though. Without the lettering, the address book (or other surface) could be used year round.

Paint: FolkArt Metallics

676 INCA GOLD

Paint: FolkArt Acrylics

420 LINEN

901 WICKER WHITE

432 SUNFLOWER

959 ENGLISH MUSTARD

945 MAPLE SYRUP

Paint: FolkArt Acrylics & Artists' Pigment

MIX 1: SUNFLOWER + PURE ORANGE (4:1)

Paint: FolkArt Artists' Pigment

628 PURE ORANGE

462 BURNT UMBER

479 PURE BLACK

PATTERN

This pattern may be hand-traced or photocopied for personal use only. This pattern is at full size.

BASECOATING

1. Using the ¼" Scotch Plastic Tape, mask off the edges of the canvas to protect the book's insides from paint. Paint the book with several coats of Linen until well covered. Use a no. 20 flat brush.

2. Transfer the pattern onto the book, as described on page 14, leaving off the lines for the deer, the small bare tree trunks and the lettering.

3. As you continue with this project, mix your paints, as you use them, with FolkArt Blending Gel to aid in blending. Pour a small puddle of gel on your palette. Dip your brush into the gel and then into the paint. Press the brush on the palette several times to mix.

SKY

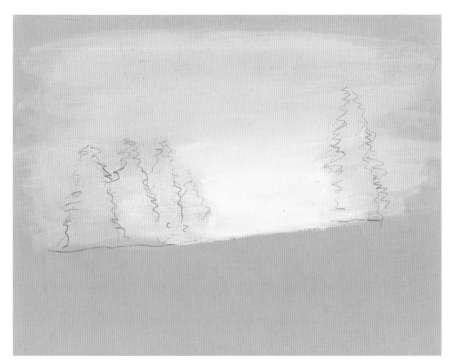

4. Paint the sky with Sunflower down to the tree line, using the no. 4 flat. Add Wicker White to the lower center part of the sky. Blend the colors.

SNOW

9. Paint the snow in horizontal streaks using Wicker White, Sunflower, Burnt Umber, Linen and Mix 1. Use a no. 4 flat brush, laying the colors on at random across the snow area and leaving some background Linen showing. You'll want to paint darker patches around the areas where the bare tree trunks and the deer will go. Use plenty of Blending Gel with your paint to keep a fluid wash. Soften the colors together somewhat by stroking horizontally with a dry brush.

TREE TRUNKS

10. Trace on the pattern of the tree trunks, the deer and the lettering, as explained on page 14. Paint the darker bare tree trunks (those traced from the pattern) using a no. 1 liner brush filled with very fluid Burnt Umber that has been thinned with water. Keep the Burnt Umber a very dark value.

TREE TRUNKS AND DEER

11. The remainder of the trunks are painted freehand, still using the no. 1 liner. Use Linen mixed with a little Burnt Umber for these lighter background trees. Pull the brush from the bottom toward the top of the canvas, lifting the brush to taper to a very fine line.

12. Add Linen and Wicker White to highlight the right side of the dark Burnt Umber trunks.

DEER

13. Paint the brown areas of the deer body with Maple Syrup on a no. 4 flat and the white areas with Wicker White on a no. 2 flat. Shade the white areas with a little Pure Black

DEER, CONTINUED

14. Add the lighter brown areas of the deer's body with English Mustard + Linen brush mixed on the no. 4 flat. Pull the brushstrokes to show the contour of the body. Using the no. 1 round brush, paint the eyes and nose with Pure Black and then lighten with Wicker White.

15. With Burnt Umber, paint the dark parts of the deer's antlers, head, body and legs. Use a no. 4 flat for the larger areas and a no. 2 flat for the smaller. Pull your brushstrokes to show the body contour. Using a no. 2 flat, lighten the upper parts of the antlers with Linen + English Mustard to show a contrast against the dark trees.

Paint the weeds with Maple Syrup and with Burnt Umber, using the no. 1 liner brush.

LETTERING

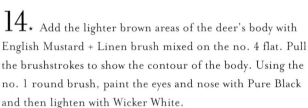

16. Paint the lettering with several coats of Inca Gold on a no. 1 round brush. Extra flourishes may be added to the letters.

17. Outline the letters with Burnt Umber on a no. 1 liner brush.

GLAZING

18. Mix Linen with enough water to make the paint thin and transparent. Using a no. 4 flat, paint over the entire design for a softening effect. To save the darkness desired on the deer and evergreen tree areas, wipe them with a paper towel or dry brush. Soften any brushstrokes with a dry brush.

COMPLETED ADDRESS BOOK

19.★ When dry, spray the painting
with one coat of FolkArt Clearcote
Acrylic Sealer.

MATERIALS

✦ **Surface**
  Wooden tray, 15" x 22½" x 3" (38cm x 57cm x 8cm), from Viking Woodcrafts. (See Resources on page 126.)

✦ **Bette Byrd Brushes**
  · no. 2 flat
  · no. 4 flat
  · no. 6 flat
  · no. 20 flat
  · no. 1 round
  · no. 1 liner
  · no. 4 fan

✦ **Other**
  · 1-inch (25mm) flat sponge

✦ **Additional Supplies**
  · wood sealer
  · 400-grit sandpaper
  · tack cloth
  · Scotch Magic Tape
  · FolkArt Blending Gel
  · white transfer paper
  · black transfer paper
  · stylus
  · palette knife
  · FolkArt Clearcote Acrylic Sealer

Dancing Snowmen Tray

This design goes a step beyond your regular snowmen. See how their arms and bodies suggest ballet dancers' movements? Even their stick fingers are held gracefully. You can also dress the snowmen however you choose.

For this project, the design is painted on the floor of a wooden tray, but there are lots of other possibilities. Sweatshirts or t-shirts are popular painting surfaces and would be perfect for these snowmen.

Paint: FolkArt Acrylics

903 TAPIOCA

640 LIGHT PERIWINKLE

403 NAVY BLUE

933 HEATHER

959 ENGLISH MUSTARD

MIX 1: TAPIOCA + LIGHT PERIWINKLE (3:4)

Paint: FolkArt Acrylics & FolkArt Artists' Pigment

MIX 2: TAPIOCA + TOUCH OF PURE ORANGE + TOUCH OF RED LIGHT

Paint: FolkArt Artists' Pigment

455 MEDIUM YELLOW

628 PURE ORANGE

629 RED LIGHT

484 BRILLIANT ULTRAMARINE

479 PURE BLACK

MIX 3: MEDIUM YELLOW + TOUCH OF BRILLIANT ULTRAMARINE

PATTERN

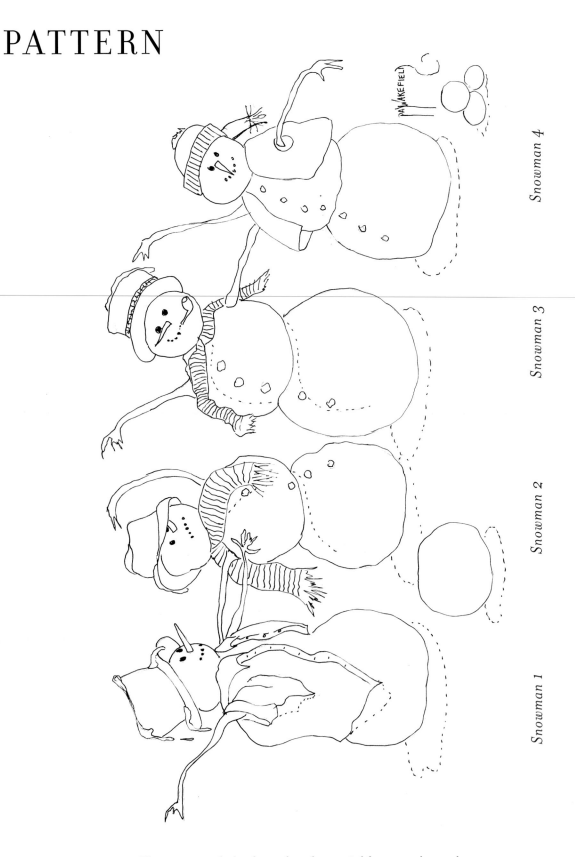

Snowman 4

Snowman 3

Snowman 2

Snowman 1

This pattern may be hand-traced or photocopied for personal use only.
Enlarge at 200%. Then enlarge again at 118% to bring up to full size.

PREPARATION AND BACKGROUND

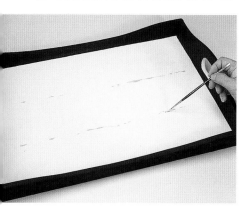

1. Seal the entire wooden tray with wood sealer. When dry, sand the tray with 400-grit sandpaper along the grain of the wood until smooth. Dust off the surface with a tack cloth.

Basecoat the floor of the tray with Tapioca on a 1-inch (25mm) flat sponge brush until well covered. Mask off the edges of the tray floor with Scotch Magic Tape. Then paint the inner and outer tray sides with Navy Blue. Use a little of any color paint and a no. 1 round brush to mark the tray floor in thirds. Eyeballing the measurement is fine.

2. Using a no. 20 flat, paint the top third of the tray floor with two coats of Navy Blue, letting the paint dry between coats. For the second coat, add a little Blending Gel. While the second coat is still wet, paint the middle third with Mix 1 + a little Blending Gel. Blend the top two-thirds with a slip-slap brushstroke, pulling the dark down and the light up. Add water on the brush to aid the blending, and add paint as needed.

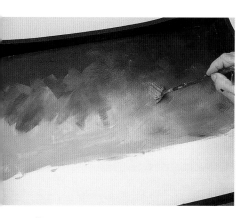

3. Finish blending with a no. 4 fan brush to give a foliage-like effect. On the left you see the blending before the fan brush was used; on the right you see blending with the fan.

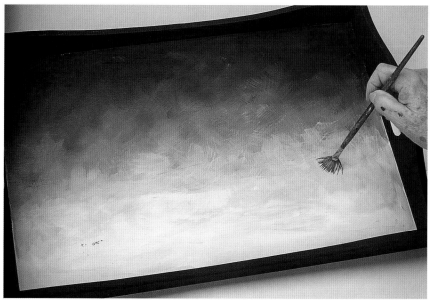

4. Paint the bottom third of the tray floor with Tapioca and a no. 20 flat brush. While this coat is wet, blend the Tapioca with Light Periwinkle. Streak with the fan brush to give a foliage effect. The right side shows pre-fan blending; the left shows fan brush blending.

BACKGROUND, CONTINUED

5. Form a horizontal line with Tapioca + Mix 1 on a no. 20 flat. You want to darken the snow a bit while keeping it lighter than the background. Blend horizontally.

6. With the no. 20 flat, apply streaks of Mix 1 horizontally across the snow. Add streaks of Mix 2.

7. Using a no. 1 liner, freehand the stick trees along the lower sky, thinning the paint with water to an ink-like consistency. Work from the bottom up. Paint some trees in Tapioca, some in Light Periwinkle and some in Light Periwinkle + Navy Blue.

8. Transfer the pattern onto the tray as explained on page 14. Use white transfer paper on the dark areas and black paper on the light areas.

SNOWMEN

9. Paint the snowmen until well-covered with several coats of Tapioca and a no. 6 flat. While the last coat is wet, add dark shading with Mix 1. Loosely blend, using a no. 20 flat for final blending.

10. At random add small amounts of Mix 2 on a no. 6 flat.

12. Paint the eyes and mouths with Pure Black on a no. 1 round brush. Add a spot of Tapioca eye highlighting to snowmen 1 and 3. (The snowmen are numbered from left to right, as marked on the pattern on page 58.)

11. Paint the snowmen's cheeks with Mix 2 on a no. 4 flat.

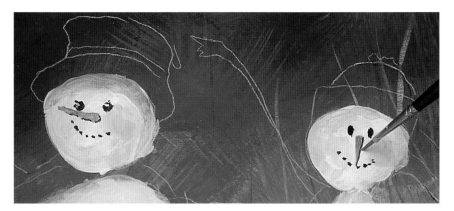

13. Paint the noses with Pure Orange on a no. 1 round. Outline one side of the noses with Pure Black.

SNOWMEN, CONTINUED

14. Paint the arms with a no. 1 round and English Mustard. Outline the bottom edges with Pure Black and the top edges with Tapioca.

15. Paint the top hats (but not the hatband) with Pure Black on a no. 4 flat. Lighten the highlighted areas with Mix 1.

16. Paint the lavender shirt with a brush mix of Heather + Tapioca, using a no. 4 flat brush. Darken with Mix 1. Lighten with Tapioca. Add just a tint of Red Light + Tapioca at random. Outline with Pure Black. Use a no. 4 flat.

17. Paint the red hat with Red Light on a no. 4 flat brush. Darken with Pure Black and highlight with Pure Orange. Paint the hatband with Pure Black. You will add the snow later.

18. Paint the green scarf with Mix 3 on a no. 4 flat brush. Darken with Brilliant Ultramarine. Lighten with Tapioca and with Pure Orange. Paint the stripes with Tapioca + Medium Yellow and with Pure Black on a no. 1 round brush.

19. Paint the plaid hatband and scarf with the no. 2 flat brush using Red Light.

20. Using a no. 1 round brush, paint stripes, alternating Medium Yellow and Mix 3.

21. Using a no. 1 round brush, paint the pipe with English Mustard and outline with Pure Black.

22. Paint the yellow hat and vest with Medium Yellow and Tapioca mixed on a no. 4 flat brush. Using the same brush, add shading with Pure Orange + English Mustard. Highlight with Tapioca.

COMPLETED
DANCING
SNOWMEN
TRAY

32. Spray the tray with two coats of
FolkArt Clearcote Acrylic Sealer, letting it
dry between coats.

 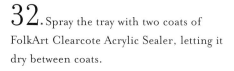

PATTERNS

Chair Seat

This pattern may be hand-traced or photocopied for personal use only.
Enlarge at 200%. Then enlarge again at 119% percent to bring up to full size.

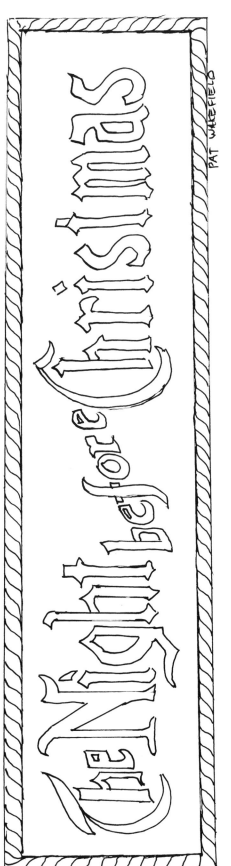

Chair Upper Back

These patterns may be hand-traced or photocopied for personal use only.
Enlarge both of these patterns at 139% to bring up to full size.

Chair Lower Back

CHAIR SEAT, CONTINUED

13. Transfer the inner circle pattern except for the moon, Santa, the reindeer, and the house details. Mask outside the perimeter of this inner circle with plastic tape.

14. Paint the sky with Dioxazine Purple on a no. 10 flat. While this is wet, add a little Tapioca to the Dioxazine Purple and lighten the lower part of the sky. Blend until smooth.

15. Paint the trees with Thicket on a no. 10 flat brush. Use a no. 4 flat with Old Ivy to show branches.

16. Paint the house in Teddy Bear Tan with a no. 4 flat brush.

17. Transfer the pattern of the moon onto the sky. Use a no. 4 flat to paint the moon with several coats of Sunflower until well covered.

18. Load a no. 2 flat brush with Tapioca thinned with a small amount of water. Paint streaks across the width of the house to resemble boards.

19. Paint the outer tree branches with Fresh Foliage on a no. 4 flat brush. With Tapioca on a no. 1 liner brush, paint the snow on the trees.

20. Paint the chimney with Christmas Red on a no. 4 flat.

21. Paint the snow on the roof, chimney and ground with Tapioca on a no. 4 flat. Add shading with Tapioca + Sterling Blue.

COMPLETED CHAIR

34. Spray over the painted area with two coats of FolkArt Clearcote Acrylic Sealer, letting it dry between coats.

Chair Seat

Chair Back

MATERIALS

✦ **Surface**
  Wooden tavern sign,
  13" x 22" (33cm x 56cm),
  from Viking Woodcrafts.
  (See Resources on page 126.)

✦ **Bette Byrd Brushes**
  • no. 4 flat
  • no. 10 flat
  • no. 20 flat
  • no. 1 round
  • no. 1 liner

✦ **Other**
  • 1-inch (25mm) flat sponge

✦ **Additional Supplies**
  • wood sealer
  • 400-grit sandpaper
  • tack cloth
  • white transfer paper
    and stylus
  • 1¼" (3.2cm) circle template
    or compass (optional)
  • FolkArt Blending Gel
  • ⅛" (3mm) Scotch Plastic
    Tape 471 Blue
  • FolkArt Clearcote
    Acrylic Sealer

"Sleigh Bells Ring" Tavern Sign

This sign could be displayed outside in a covered place by your front door or in a selected place inside.

The greenery is balsam fir tree branches, which have short stubby needles. We often see this variety for sale on Christmas tree lots.

Paint: FolkArt Acrylics

953 CAMEL

959 ENGLISH MUSTARD

924 THICKET

901 WICKER WHITE

432 SUNFLOWER

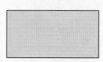
736 SCHOOL BUS YELLOW

930 PRIMROSE

436 ENGINE RED

922 BAYBERRY

723 MYSTIC GREEN

MIX 1: ENGLISH MUSTARD + CAMEL (2:1)

Paint: FolkArt Acrylics & FolkArt Artists' Pigment

MIX 2: MIX 1 + RED LIGHT + THICKET (1:1:1)

MIX 3: YELLOW OCHRE + WICKER WHITE (1:1:1)

Paint: FolkArt Artists' Pigment

917 YELLOW OCHRE

628 PURE ORANGE

629 RED LIGHT

463 DIOXAZINE PURPLE

462 BURNT UMBER

PATTERNS

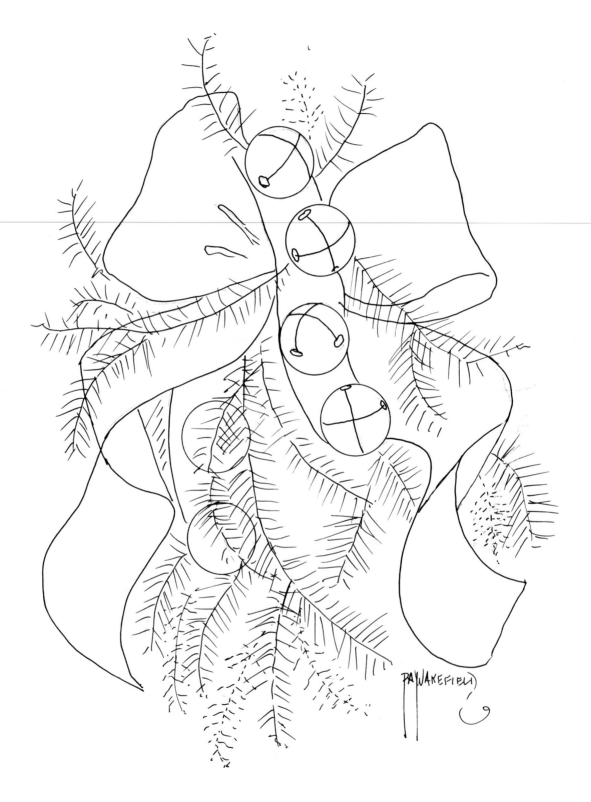

This pattern may be hand-traced or photocopied for personal use only. Enlarge at 156% to bring up to full size.

PAT WAKEFIELD

Upper Frame

Are You Listening

PAT WAKEFIELD

Lower Frame

These patterns may be hand-traced or photocopied for personal use only.
Enlarge both patterns at 169% to bring up to full size.

PREPARATION AND BACKGROUND

1. Remove screws to separate the oval from the frame. Seal all wood with wood sealer. When dry, sand with 400-grit sandpaper. Remove the dust with a tack cloth.

2. Using a 1-inch (25mm) flat sponge brush, paint the oval with several coats of Mix 1 until well covered. Then paint the vertical frame strips with Mix 1 until well covered. Paint the horizontal frame strips with several coats of Thicket until well covered.

3. Transfer the patterns onto the wood as explained on page 14. You can transfer the branch lines overlapping the bells and ribbon after painting those elements. Transfer the bell outlines. You may want to use a 1¼" (3.2cm) circle template or a compass to help you get perfect circles.

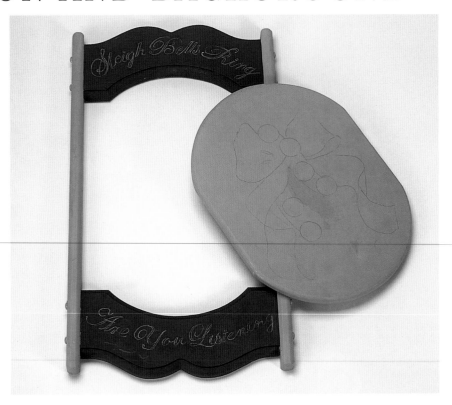

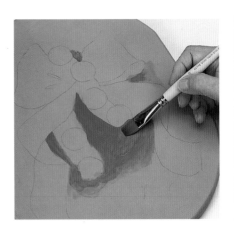

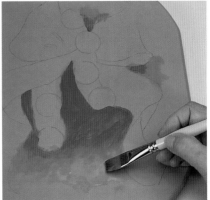

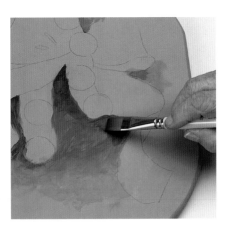

4. On the oval board, fill in the background between pattern lines with Mix 2 + a little Blending Gel on a no. 20 flat. Apply two coats.

5. Brush-mix your Mix 1 + Mix 2 + a little Blending Gel with a no. 20 flat brush and apply to the outer edge of the background you just painted. Blend.

6. Brush-mix Thicket + Burnt Umber on the no. 20 flat to add further shading to the background.

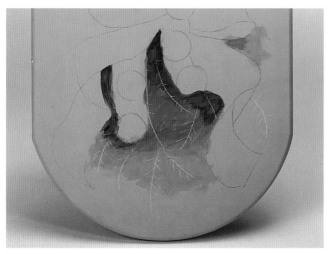

7. Draw (or redraw) the pattern lines for the branches as shown in the photo. Only a general line is given for pine needles. The dotted branch lines on the pattern indicate pine branch shadows. These may be transferred or painted freehand.

8. Paint the pine branch shadows with Mix 2 thinned with water to a transparent consistency. Use a no. 1 liner.

RIBBON

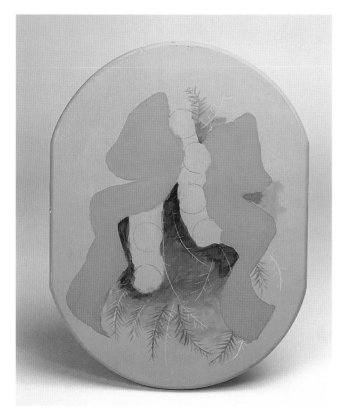

9. Basecoat the ribbon with several coats of Primrose and a no. 20 flat brush.

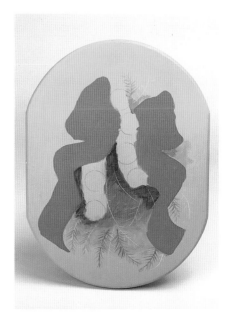

10. Basecoat the ribbon again with Red Light on a no. 20 flat. Apply two coats so that the ribbon is well covered.

RIBBON, CONTINUED

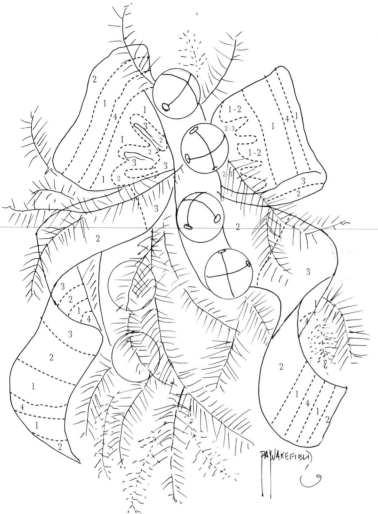

COLOR MAP

Key To Color Map

1 - Red Light

2 - Engine Red

3 - Dioxazine Purple

4 - Highlighting

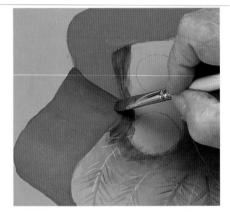

13. Add a stripe of Dioxazine Purple + Blending Gel next to the Engine Red. Blend the stripes.

11. The next three colors are laid across the ribbon width one at a time with a no. 10 flat. Add Blending Gel to each color, and blend each color with the previous one while the paint is still wet. Work one section of the ribbon at a time, using the diagram to help you with color placement.

Highlighting is done in several steps, using Primrose and Wicker White. It's applied on portions of the already painted Red Light stripes.

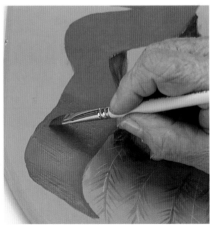

12. Start with a stripe of Red Light and then a stripe of Engine Red. Remember to add Blending Gel to each color. Blend these two stripes.

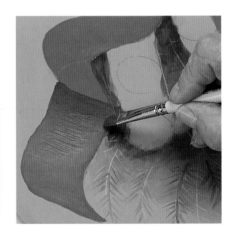

14. To achieve a smoother effect, repeat the striping and blending of the same colors in this same section.

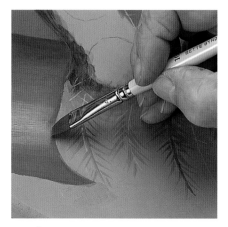

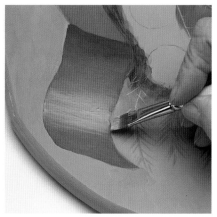

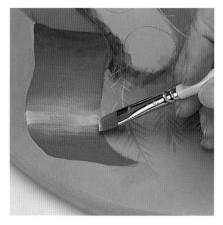

15. In the same ribbon section, start to add highlights with a basecoat of Primrose + Blending Gel on a no. 10 flat.

16. While the paint is wet, add Primrose + Wicker White + a little Blending Gel.

17. Add Wicker White alone to the lightest areas. Go through the striping, blending and highlighting sequence on other portions of the ribbon, working section by section.

The bow folds are handled a bit differently. See the next three steps and refer to the color map on page 86.

BOW FOLDS

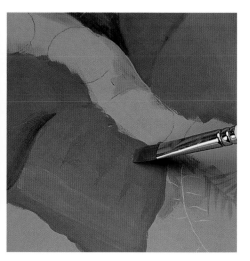

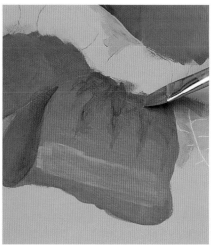

18. Block in the bow folds with Engine Red and a no. 10 flat. Do not blend.

19. Darken the folds with Engine Red + Dioxazine Purple. Blend to soften the colors.

20. Make a transparent mixture of Blending Gel + Engine Red and apply over the folds to smooth out the colors.

LEATHER STRAP

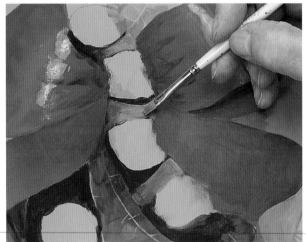

22. With the no. 4 flat, highlight the upper strap with English Mustard mixed with a little Wicker White.

21. Basecoat the leather strap with Burnt Umber, using a no. 4 flat.

BELLS

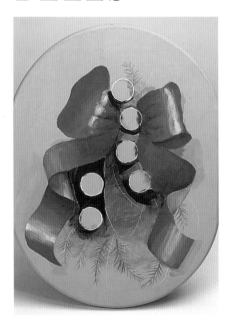

23. Use your circle template or compass to retrace the bells, making sure they are exact 1¼" (3.2cm) circles. Basecoat all the bells with Yellow Ochre on a no. 4 flat.

24. Using the no. 4 flat, add Blending Gel over the basecoat one bell at a time. While this is damp, apply the reflecting and shading colors—Engine Red, Mystic Green, Burnt Umber, School Bus Yellow, Sunflower, and Wicker White— adding water to each as it is put on. Randomly spot these colors and let them run together.

Slightly soften with a dry no. 4 flat brush. The white spots may need to be added a second time.

25. Notice that the bells under the branches use more of the dark colors. Those in the center show more reflecting colors.

Dry the bells with a hair dryer. Transfer the pattern of the bell openings or just draw them in freehand. These openings are painted with Pure Black and a no. 1 liner.

BALSAM BRANCHES

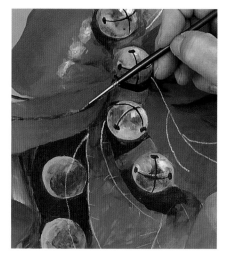

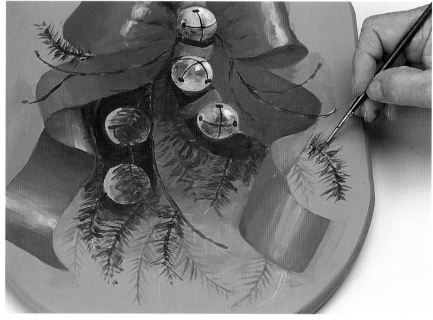

26. Trace on pine branches that overlap the ribbons and the bells. Needles do not need to be traced. Paint a Burnt Umber line for the branches with a no. 1 round. At random add spots of Pure Orange.

27. The pine needles should be done freehand, some overlapping others and some placed at different angles. First paint the needles on the branches that are underneath, using Thicket on a no. 1 round brush. Keep the needles rather short and blunt, without much taper.

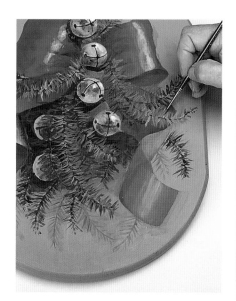

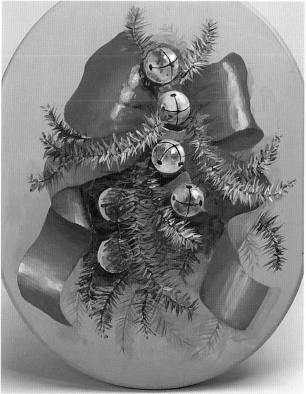

29. Add some needles of Bayberry + a little Sunflower on the highlighted branches,

28. For the needles on the remaining branches, start with Thicket, then Mystic Green and then Bayberry. They should have a random look.

FRAME STRIPING AND LETTERING

30. Mask off the upper and lower horizontal frame edge with ⅛" (3mm) Scotch Plastic Tape. First lay the tape ⅛" (3mm) from the outer edge and then place another strip ⅛" (3mm) from the first tape.

31. Fill in between the taped edges with a small amount of Primrose, using a no. 4 flat brush. Apply two coats. Add two layers of Red Light, applying only a small amount at a time to avoid paint running under the tape.

32. Peel off the tape.

33. Paint the lettering with a no. 1 liner brush and Mix 3 thinned with water. Press on the brush for the wider places in the lettering and lift the brush as the line tapers out narrowly. When the lettering is dry, clean off the transfer lines with water on a brush.

COMPLETED TAVERN SIGN

34. Spray the entire project with two coats of FolkArt Clearcote Acrylic Sealer, letting it dry after each coat. Assemble the oval and the frame.

MATERIALS

✦ **Surface**
Wooden sled 7" x 12 3/4"
(18cm x 32cm) with metal
runners, from Viking
Woodcrafts. (See Resources
on page 126.)

✦ **Bette Byrd Brushes**
· no. 4 flat
· no. 6 flat
· no. 1 round
· no. 1 liner
· 1/4-inch (6mm)
Pat Wakefield's Deer Foot

✦ **Other**
· 1-inch (25mm)
flat sponge brush

✦ **Additional Supplies**
· wood sealer
· 400-grit sandpaper
· tack cloth
· white transfer paper
and stylus
· FolkArt Blending Gel
· paper towels
· FolkArt Clearcote Acrylic
Sealer
· Rust-oleum Spray Metal
Primer
· Rust-oleum Spray Enamel,
Gloss Black
· 1/4" (6mm) straight-blade
screwdriver

PROJECT **8**

Teddy Bear Sled

Teddy bears are such fun to decorate with, especially

at Christmas. I named this one "Nippy," since he's

dressed in his ski sweater, ready for the season. Nippy

could also be painted on a sweatshirt or child's toy.

Use your imagination.

Paint: FolkArt Acrylics

901 WICKER WHITE

450 PARCHMENT

432 SUNFLOWER

417 TEDDY BEAR
BROWN

612 HOLIDAY RED

441 STERLING
BLUE

924 THICKET

MIX 1: WICKER
WHITE + THICKET
(3:1)

MIX 2: WICKER
WHITE + STERLING
BLUE (3:1)

Paint: FolkArt Artists' Pigment

917 YELLOW
OCHRE

628 PURE ORANGE

629 RED LIGHT

462 BURNT UMBER

479 PURE BLACK

PATTERN

This pattern may be hand-traced or photocopied for personal use only. Enlarge at 134% to bring up to full size.

PREPARATION

PAINTING ORDER

Painting the Sections in Order

Some areas of the teddy bear are overlapped by others. Paint from the background areas first and then work forward so the overlapping fuzzy edges of the fur will show. Refer to the the section painting order list below:

1. Right ear
2. Face
3. Hat (no design)
4. Left ear
5. Sweater (no design)
6. Lower face edge (touch up)
7. Hat and sweater designs
8. Front paws
9. Rear legs
10. Rear paws

Painting the Colors in Order

Stipple the teddy bear fur colors in the same order from section to section, starting with the medium value. Then, one by one, add the medium dark value, the darkest value, the medium light value and finally the highlight. The swatches below show the difference between value order and painting order.

 3  2  1  4  5

Color Painting Order: From left to right you see the fur colors from darkest to lightest value. The numbers indicate the painting order: (1) Yellow Ochre/medium value (2) Teddy Bear Brown/medium dark value) (3) Burnt Umber/dark value (4) Sunflower/medium light value (5) Parchment/light value.

1. Apply wood sealer to the wooden parts of the sled. Sand with 400-grit sandpaper. Clean off the sanding dust with a tack cloth. Basecoat with Holiday Red on a 1-inch (25mm) flat sponge brush. Add several more coats of Holiday Red until well covered. Transfer the pattern as described on page 14, leaving off the hat and sweater designs.

RIGHT EAR

2. (left) Pat Wakefield's Deer Foot Brush by Bette Byrd (see page 11) is the perfect stippling tool for painting the teddy bear's fur. Dip the edge of the Deer Foot into the Blending Gel and then load the longest hair of the brush with Yellow Ochre. Dab the brush on a paper towel to remove some overloaded paint. Then stipple the paint onto the surface with a pouncing motion and fill in the entire ear.

3. (right) Wipe the brush on a paper towel. Then, following the technique described in step 2, stipple with Teddy Bear Brown.

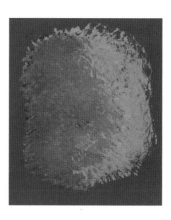

RIGHT EAR, CONTINUED

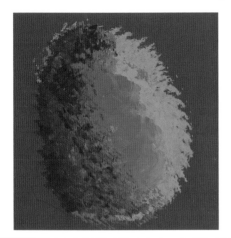

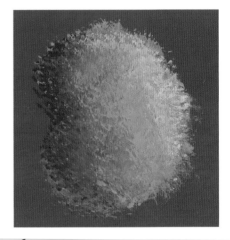

4. Wipe off the brush and repeat the procedure using Burnt Umber.

5. Wipe off the brush and then continue to stipple over the paint to blend the colors. Use a light touch here.

6. Wipe the brush and stipple on Sunflower.

FACE

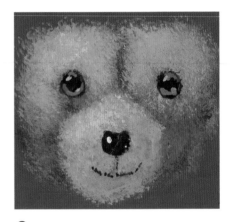

7. Wipe the brush and stipple on Parchment. Blend the colors, but keep a separation of the lights from the darks. Keep a fuzzy effect along the outer edge by using just a few hairs of the brush to stipple.

For the rest of the fur sections, follow the procedure in steps 2 through 7. Refer to the section painting order on page 95 for a reminder of what to paint next.

8. Notice that all parts of the face don't have all the color values. For example, you will lay some dark values (Burnt Umber) where the eyes will be placed. On the other hand, the lightest color (Parchment) shows the highlights created by an unseen light source shining from above.

Paint the eyes, eyelashes and mouth using a no. 1 round brush and Pure Black.

9. Lighten around the outer edge of the eyes using Pure Black + Wicker White on a no. 1 round brush. Using the same brush, paint the highlights with Wicker White. Soften these highlights with a dry brush.

HINT

By keeping the side edges of each part of the face dark and the center light, you create rounding to the head parts.

HAT AND SWEATER

10. Use a no. 6 flat to paint the hat and the sweater with several coats of Parchment until well covered. While the Parchment is still wet, add the shading. Dip the corner of the no. 6 flat into the Blending Gel and then into the paint to keep it wet and allow softer blending. Use Mix 1 first and then Mix 2. Refer to the photo on the left for placement of shading. Blend somewhat, but smoothness is not necessary.

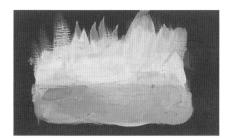

11. Paint a ³/₈" (1cm) stripe along the bottom edges of the hat, sweater and sweater sleeves with Mix 2 on a no. 4 flat.

12. Using a no. 1 round, paint Wicker White ribbing lines to the sweater and sweater sleeve edges.

13. The designs on the hat and sweater can easily be painted freehand. The red hat stripes are Holiday Red with some highlighting of Red Light. The Green lines on the hat are Thicket. Use a no. 1 round.

14. The ball on the top of the hat is painted in lines done with a no. 1 liner brush. Use Red Light, Pure Orange, Holiday Red and Burnt Umber. Paint the ball's shadow with Mix 1 on a no. 1 round.

SWEATER, CONTINUED

15. The trees on the sweater are Mix 1. The red dots are Holiday Red. Use a no. 1 round.

Then use the Deer Foot to stipple in the paws and legs as explained on pages 95-96.

HOLLY

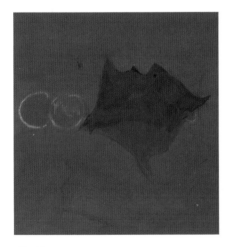

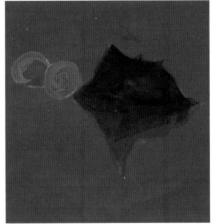

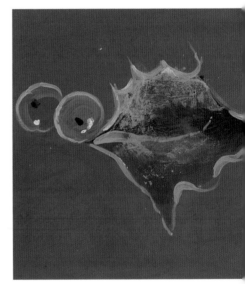

16. Using a no. 4 flat, paint the holly leaves with Thicket.

17. Add Pure Black shading. Then, with a no. 1 round, paint the berries with Holiday Red and lighten with Pure Orange.

18. Highlight the leaves with Sunflower + Parchment on the no. 4 flat. With the no. 1 round, add a Parchment highlight to the berries and a Pure Black dot. With the no. 1 liner, outline the berries and holly with Yellow Ochre + Parchment.

COMPLETED SLED

19. When the paint is dry, spray the wood with two coats of FolkArt Clearcote Acrylic Sealer, letting it dry between coats.

Paint the runners with Rust-oleum Spray Metal Primer. Let dry. Then paint them with Rust-oleum Spray Gloss Black Enamel. Follow the instructions on the cans.

When dry, attach the runners to the sled with a ¼" (6mm) straight-blade screwdriver.

Old World Santa Stockings

I have created a collection of Old World Santas, each from a real model representing a different country. I prefer to paint these faces using tube oils.

Santa O'Claus is just a figment of my imagination. He looks to me to be a fine, jolly old fellow from Ireland who could easily be a Santa Claus. I used my brother, Larry Kennedy, as my model. Larry is Irish, and he certainly has many of the qualities that would be desirable for a Santa. He's a warm, generous person, well-liked by everyone. The name "Santa O'Claus" suits his nature.

Sir Christmas became popular in England during the Protestant Reformation. At that time it was improper to celebrate anything having to do with Catholic saints such as Saint Nicholas, patron saint of Christmas. Observances of Christmas festivities were forbidden by government order. As a celebration for the common people, Sir Christmas visited homes not to bring gifts but to sit a while by the fire.

Pat Wakefield's brother, Larry Kennedy, served as model for Santa O'Claus.

Jim Byrne, Pat Wakefield's friend, is the model for Sir Christmas.

My painting shows the way I'd like Sir Christmas to look. The model, Jim Byrne, is a special friend of mine who also has the character traits for his role. He's a warm, friendly, big-hearted man, well-loved by many.

Both these Old World Santa stockings use the tube oil palette on the following page. Although instructions for "Sir Christmas" do not include step-by-step photos, you'll find that the painting process and techniques are much like those for "Santa O' Claus." Painting packets for other Old World Santas are available through my Web site (see Resources, page 126).

(opposite left) Santa O'Claus
(opposite right) Sir Christmas

MATERIALS

✦ **Surface**

Fabric stocking (Follow directions on page 104.)

✦ **Bette Byrd Brushes**
- no. 2 flat
- no. 4 flat
- no. 6 flat
- no. 20 flat
- no. 1 round
- no. 1 liner
  (Santa O'Claus only)
- no. 6/0 liner
- ¹/₂-inch (13mm) whisk brush

✦ **Additional Supplies**
- 18" x 24" (46cm x 61cm) cotton fabric, such as muslin, poplin or canvas
- paper-cutting scissors
- fabric shears
- sewing machine or needle and thread
- steam iron and pressing cloth
- FolkArt Textile Medium
- hair dryer
- 400-grit sandpaper
- tack cloth
- Scotch Magic Tape
- white transfer paper and stylus
- cobalt siccative drier (optional)
- Winsor & Newton Blending & Glazing Medium
- paper towel
- colorless paint thinner for oil paints
- Grumbacher Picture Varnish
- 19" x 6" (48cm x 15cm) imitation fur
- hot glue gun
- 10" (25cm) of ¹/₂" (1.3cm) red grosgrain ribbon

Paint: Tube Oils

TITANIUM WHITE

CADMIUM YELLOW LIGHT

YELLOW OCHRE

CADMIUM RED LIGHT

ALIZARIN CRIMSON

ULTRAMARINE BLUE

BURNT UMBER

IVORY BLACK

MIX 1: YELLOW OCHRE + ALIZARIN CRIMSON + BURNT UMBER + TITANIUM WHITE (2:2:2:1)

MIX 2: TITANIUM WHITE + CADMIUM RED LIGHT + CADMIUM YELLOW LIGHT (1:1:4)

MIX 3: IVORY BLACK + CADMIUM YELLOW LIGHT + ULTRAMARINE BLUE (1:2:3)

MIX 4: MIX 3 + TITANIUM WHITE + CADMIUM YELLOW LIGHT (2:2:2)

MIX 5: MIX 3 + ALIZARIN CRIMSON + TITANIUM WHITE (4:2:1)

Paint: Folk Art Acrylic

937 DAPPLE GRAY

HINT

Using oils on these Santas seems to result in a richer look than painting with acrylics. Also, the blendability of oils helps achieve a softer look. However, too much blending will make Santa seem young, so keep a little choppiness.

These paintings could be done in acrylics if you're skilled in this medium. You'll need to match the paint mixes to your acrylic color.

"SANTA O'CLAUS" PATTERN

This pattern may be hand-traced or photocopied for personal use only.
Enlarge at 200%. Then enlarge again at 117% to bring up to full size.

103

PREPARATION

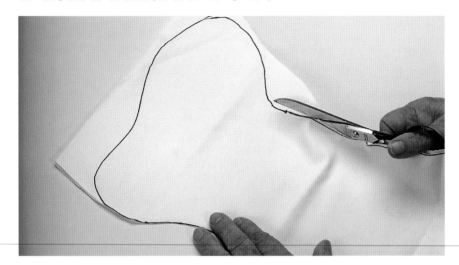

1. Take one piece of cotton fabric (muslin, poplin, canvas, etc.) measuring 18" x 24" (46cm x 61cm). The fabric should be folded in half to create two layers of 18" x 12" (46cm x 30cm) fabric. Cut out the enlarged stocking pattern and use it to outline the stocking pattern shape on one side of the folded fabric. With the fabric still folded, cut out two stocking pieces.

2. Machine or hand stitch the stocking pieces together with a ¼" (6mm) seam.

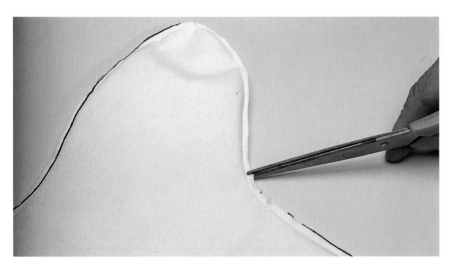

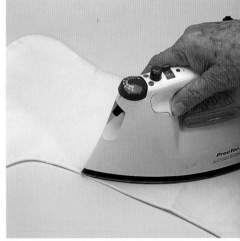

3. Clip the seams at the curves.

4. Turn the stocking right side out, making sure the seams are pushed all the way out to create a smooth stocking-shaped contour. Steam iron.

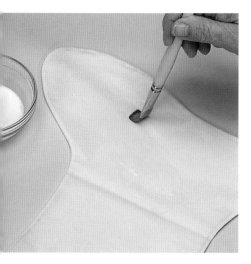

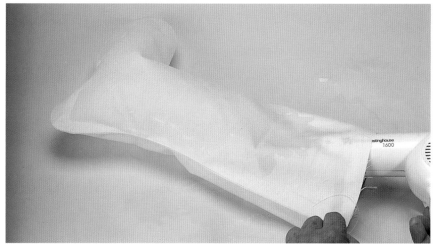

5. Using a no. 20 flat, coat the fabric front and back with Textile Medium. This will stiffen and waterproof the fabric.

6. Dry the stocking with a hair dryer, directing the flow inside and outside the stocking. Keep the fabric smooth. Add another coat of Textile Medium and repeat the drying procedure. When the second coat is dry, steam iron the stocking again, using a pressing cloth.

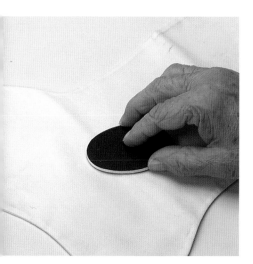

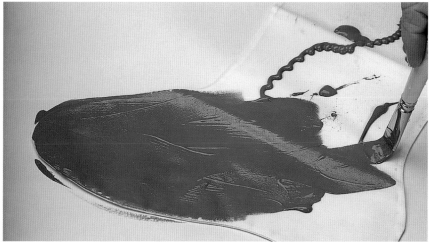

7. Sand lightly with 400-grit sandpaper. Remove the sanding dust with a tack cloth.

8. Paint the stocking front and back with two coats of Dapple Gray and a no. 20 flat. Dry with a blow dryer, sanding lightly after each coat and removing the sanding dust with a tack cloth.

PREPARATION, CONTINUED

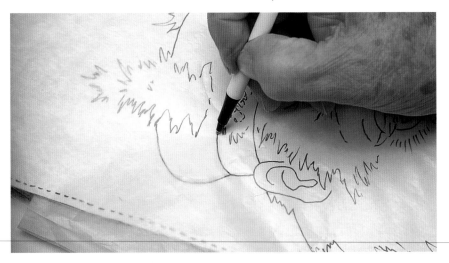

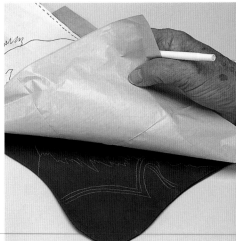

9. Tape the Santa pattern to the stocking. Slip white transfer paper between the pattern and the stocking, and trace the pattern with a pen or stylus.

You may want to place waxed paper over the pattern before you begin tracing, as I've done here. The impressions from the pen or stylus enable you to see which lines you've traced.

10. Wax paper may keep you from missing or repeating tracing lines, but it doesn't guarantee that your transfer paper is in place. So periodically check under the pattern to make sure the lines are transferring.

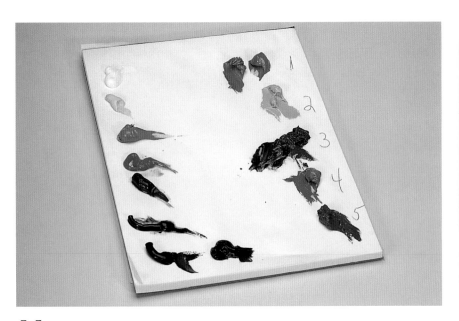

11. When painting with oils, I prefer disposable palette paper to a permanent palette. (See explanation of palettes on page 10.)

Place your unmixed colors down one side of the palette. Prepare the paint mixtures on a separate sheet of palette paper and then transfer them to your main palette. Label the mixes with their numbers.

HINT

You may choose to use cobalt siccative drier, which will promote drying of tube oils. Use only a drop in each paint mixture on your palette.

BACKGROUND

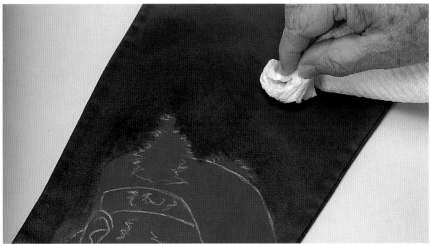

12. Using a no. 6 flat, pick up a small amount of Glazing Medium with Mix 3. Paint the background first, from the shoulders to about 3" (8cm) above the head. Turn the stocking as needed to keep your hand out of the paint.

13. Rub the wet paint with a paper towel to soften the edges and remove some paint, letting the basecoat show through.

14. With a brush mixture of Mix 3 + Ivory Black, slip-slap the area above the head to darken. Use the no. 20 flat to blend the color until soft but splotchy.

EYES AND FOREHEAD

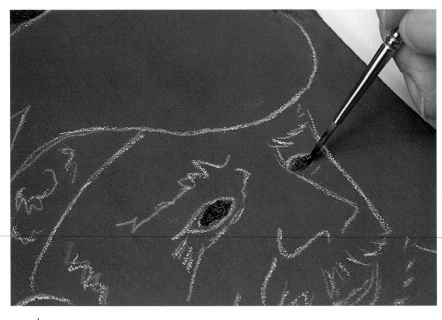

15. Basecoat the eyes with a brush mix of Ultramarine Blue + Ivory Black on the no. 1 round.

16. Paint the upper and lower eyelids with Mix 2, using the no. 1 round. Add a touch of Cadmium Red Light just under each eye.

HINT

Avoid overblending as you paint Santa's face and he will appear older, with wrinkled skin.

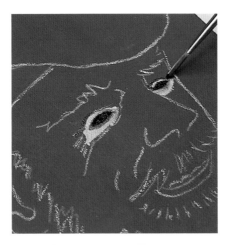

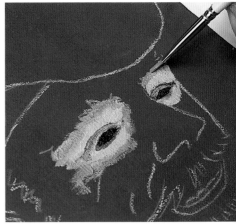

17. Still using the no. 1 round, outline the eyelids with Burnt Umber, blending slightly.

18. With Mix 2 on a no. 2 flat, paint the flesh above the upper lids and below the lower lids. Darken with Mix 1. Blend slightly. The left eye shows this step completed.

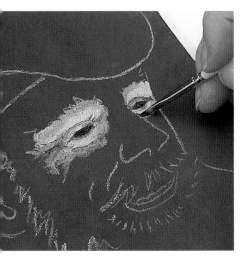

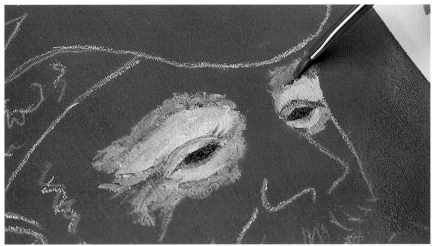

19. Using the no. 2 flat with Mix 2, paint the wrinkle areas beside and beneath the eyes. Darken with Burnt Umber.

20. Paint the eyebrows with Mix 1 on the no. 2 flat. Add Burnt Umber shading just under the eyebrows and blend slightly.

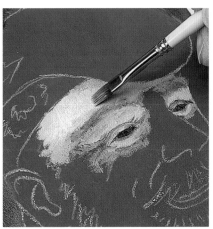

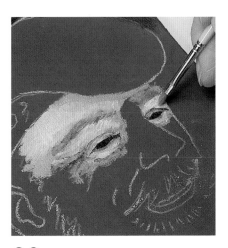

21. Paint the light area of the forehead with Mix 2, using a no. 4 flat. Paint the dark area using Mix 1. Add additional Titanium White in the lightest area of the forehead.

22. With a no. 6 flat, blend this whole area slightly, leaving it somewhat splotchy.

23. Using a no. 2 flat, apply Titanium White on the upper and lower eyelids and between the eyebrows and eyelids.

NOSE

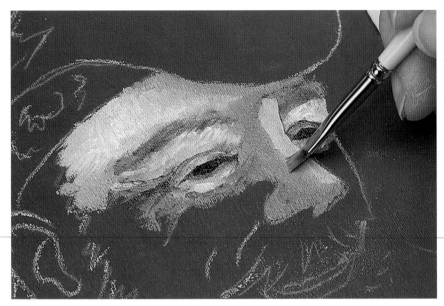

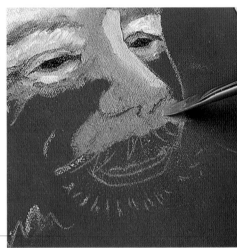

24. Following the shadows and highlights on the photograph, take a no. 4 flat and apply Mix 2 for the light areas and Mix 1 for the dark areas. Blend only slightly.

25. Paint the flesh under the nose with Mix 1 and the no. 4 flat.

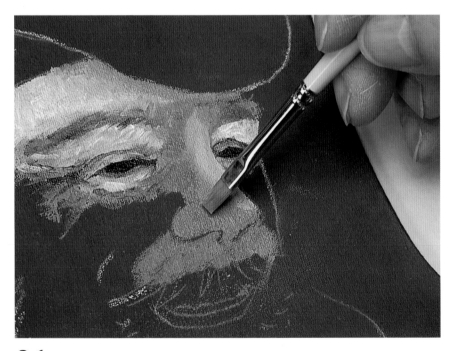

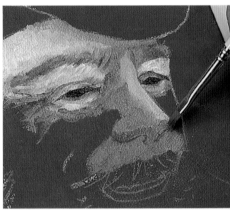

26. Brush-mix Cadmium Red Light with Mix 1 and paint over the darker parts of the nose, pulling the color into the forehead.

27. With a no. 4 flat, add Burnt Umber just above the nostrils and reinforce the wrinkles between the eyebrows.

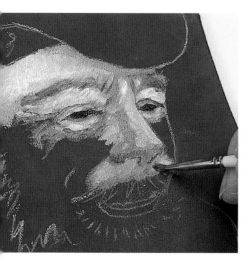

28. With a no. 2 flat, apply Titanium White to the nose highlights. Blend slightly to create a splotchy look. Add a bit of Titanium White under the nose.

29. With Burnt Umber on a no. 1 liner, paint the shadows cast under the nostrils and to the right of the nose.

CHEEKS

30. With a no. 4 flat, fill in the highlight area of the cheeks with Mix 2. Fill the remainder of the cheeks and up the side of the face with Mix 1.

31. With a no. 6 flat, blend the areas you just painted.

CHEEKS, CONTINUED

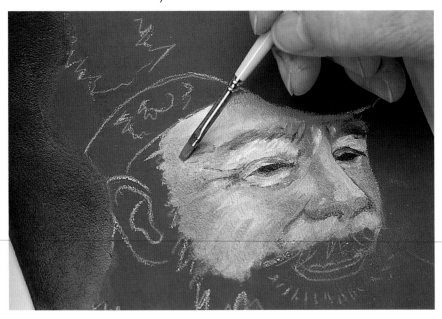

32. With a no. 2 flat, add Cadmium Red Light in the ruddier areas and blend.

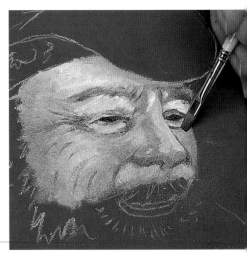

33. Using a no. 1 round with Mix 1 and Burnt Umber, paint the wrinkles around the eyes and on the left side of the face. Then blend the whole cheek slightly.

34. Reinforce the highlight on the cheek with Titanium White on a no. 2 flat. Blend.

EAR AND MOUTH

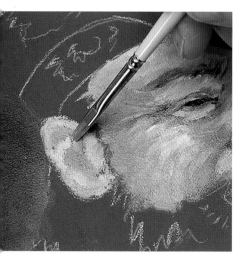

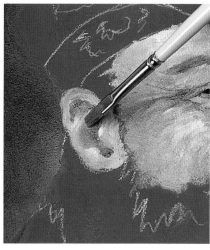

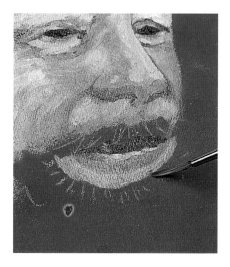

35. Paint the ear with Mix 1 on a no. 2 flat.

36. Still with the no. 2 flat, add shading with Burnt Umber and highlighting with Titanium White.

37. Using a no. 1 round, paint the teeth with Mix 1 and Titanium White. Darken with Burnt Umber. Paint the inside of the mouth with a mixture of Burnt Umber and Ivory Black. Paint the lower lip with Mix 1 + Alizarin Crimson + Burnt Umber. Paint under the lip with Mix 1 + Mix 2.

HAT AND COLLAR

38. Basecoat the hat, collar and the remainder of the background with Mix 3 on a no. 6 flat, using a slip-slap stroke to keep a loose effect. Lighten with Mix 4 on the upper hat and the collar points. Blend, using a slip-slap stroke, with a no. 20 flat.

HAIR

39. Paint the hair on the beard, mustache and head with a no. 4 flat and Mix 5 + Titanium White.

40. Use a ¹/₂-inch (13mm) whisk brush to blend Titanium White in the direction the hair grows.

41. Add lines of Titanium White thinned with paint thinner to an ink-like consistency. Apply very fine lines to the eyebrows with a no. 6/0 liner. Add thicker lines to the beard with a no. 1 liner.

HATBAND AND TRIM

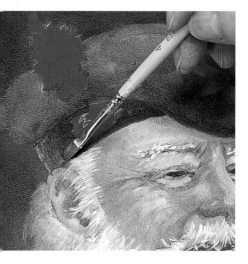

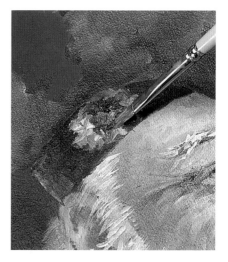

42. With a no. 6 flat, paint the hatband in Ivory Black. Lighten with Titanium White.

43. Using a no. 4 flat, paint the emblem with Yellow Ochre.

44. Dab in splotches of Ivory Black, Cadmium Red Light, Titanium White and Cadmium Yellow Light with a no. 4 flat.

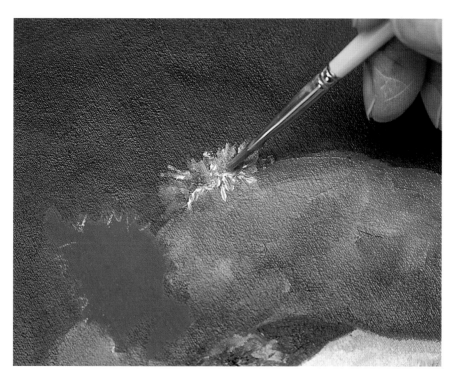

46. Using the chisel edge of a no. 4 flat, paint the hat tassel with streaks of Titanium White and Ivory Black. Blend some of the streaks to gray.

45. For the pompom on the hat, start with streaks of Yellow Ochre. Add streaks of Burnt Umber and Titanium White. Use the no. 4 flat.

VEST

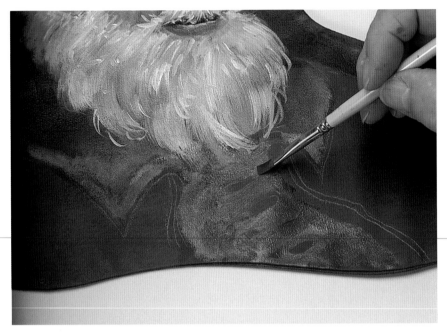

47. Basecoat the vest, using a no. 6 flat and Cadmium Red Light. Darken with Alizarin Crimson.

48. Still using the no. 6 flat, darken further with Burnt Umber. Use a slip-slap stroke to blend, but don't overdo it.

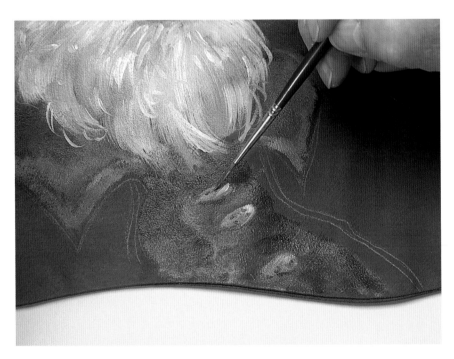

49. Using the no. 6 flat, paint the buttons with Yellow Ochre. Darken with Burnt Umber. Highlight with Titanium White. Use a no. 1 liner to paint the buttonholes with Burnt Umber.

COAT

50. Fill in the remainder of the coat with Mix 3, using a no. 6 flat brush. Lighten with Mix 4. Add shadows with Ivory Black. Use a slip-slap stroke to keep a loose effect.

51. Paint the coat trim with Yellow Ochre on a no. 6 flat.

HINT

Normal drying time for oils is two weeks. With cobalt siccative drier, they will dry overnight. Acrylics dry in one hour.

FINISHING

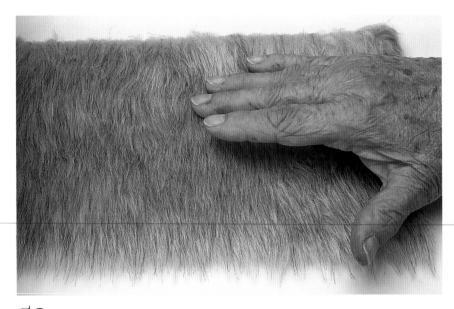

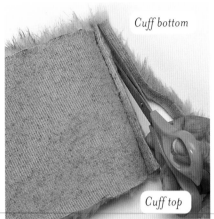

Cuff bottom

Cuff top

52. When the paints have dried, spray the stocking with Grumbacher Picture Varnish.

Cut a 19" x 6" (48cm x 15cm) piece of imitation fur. Cut the fabric from the back side, being careful to cut only the backing and not the fur. Notice that the fur has a nap. When you attach the cuff to the stocking, this nap should point down.

53. Place right sides together and stitch a side seam that runs at an angle from ½" (1.3cm) at the bottom (where the fur extends beyond the fur backing) to 1" (2.5cm) at the top. Trim the seam to ½" (1.3cm).

54. Hot glue about 2" (5cm) of the narrow end of the cuff inside the stocking, placing wrong sides together and keeping the cuff seam allowance open. Fold the fur over the stocking to form the cuff.

55. Cut a 10" (25cm) length of ½" (1.3cm) red grosgrain ribbon. Fold the ribbon in half and hot glue the ends to the inside of the cuff for a hanger.

COMPLETED
SANTA O'CLAUS STOCKING

"SIR CHRISTMAS" PATTERN

This pattern may be hand-traced or photocopied for personal use only.
Enlarge at 200%. Then enlarge again at 110% to bring up to full size.

GETTING STARTED

1. See page 101 for the origin of Sir Christmas. The process and technique for painting this Santa-like character are much like those used with "Santa O'Claus." Refer to page 102 for palette, brushes and other materials. See pages 104-106 for stocking preparation and assembly. Do not transfer the holly leaf-and-shadow pattern lines until the forehead is dry.

2. Using a no. 6 flat, pick up a small amount of Glazing Medium with Mix 3. Paint from the top of the head to about 3" (8cm) above it and from the sides of the head and shoulders to the outside edges of the stocking. Soften the upper edge by rubbing it with a paper towel to remove some paint, letting the Dapple Gray basecoat show through.

3. Darken the area above the head and on each side of the head and body with Mix 3 + Ivory Black. Blend with a slip-slap stroke, using a no. 20 flat, until the area is soft but splotchy.

EYES

4. Using a no. 1 round, paint the irises with Ultramarine Blue + Ivory Black + Titanium White. Lighten the lower part of the irises with Titanium White.

5. Paint the white of the eyes with Titanium White + a touch of Burnt Umber. Add a Titanium White highlight on the white of the left eye.

6. Paint the pupils with Ivory Black. Outline the irises and add eyelash lines with the same color.

7. Paint the upper and lower eyelids with Mix 2, still using the no. 1 round. Outline the eyelids with Burnt Umber and then blend.

8. Paint the flesh above and below the lids with a no. 2 flat and Mix 2. Darken with Mix 1. Blend slightly.

9. Paint the wrinkled area below the left eye with Mix 2 on a no. 4 flat. Pull the wrinkles at angles both up and down.

10. Paint the eyebrows with Mix 1 on a no. 1 round.

FOREHEAD

11. Paint the light forehead area with Mix 2, using a no. 4 flat. Paint the dark forehead area with Mix 1. Add additional Titanium White in the lightest area of the forehead. Blend this whole area only slightly, leaving it somewhat splotchy.

12. Add the wrinkles using Mix 1 + Burnt Umber on a no. 1 round. Blend to soften the lines.

NOSE AND RIGHT CHEEK

13. Paint the nose and the flesh under the nose with a no. 4 flat brush. Use Mix 2 for the light areas and Mix 1 for the dark areas. Blend only slightly. Add a tint of Alizarin Crimson + Burnt Umber to the nose.

14. Basecoat the right cheek with Mix 1 on a no. 4 flat. Darken the shadow next to the nose and mouth with Mix 1 + Burnt Umber.

HINT

Avoid overblending as you paint Sir Christmas's face and he will appear older, with wrinkled skin.

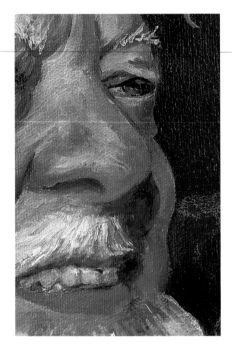

LEFT CHEEK AND EAR

15. With Mix 2 on a no. 4 flat, paint the highlight area of the left cheek. Fill the remainder of the cheek with Mix 1. Add Cadmium Red Light in the ruddier areas. Deepen with a bit of Alizarin Crimson + Burnt Umber.

16. Paint the wrinkles with Mix 1 + Burnt Umber on a no. 1 round brush. Blend this whole cheek area slightly. Reinforce the highlight on the cheek with Titanium White.

17. Paint the ear with Mix 1 on a no. 2 flat. Add dark shading with Burnt Umber. Add the light areas with Titanium White.

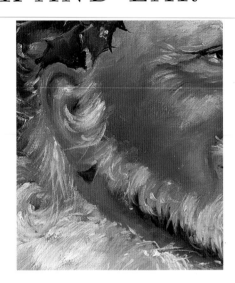

TEETH AND LIPS

18. Using a no. 1 round, paint the teeth with Mix 1 + Titanium White. Darken with Burnt Umber. Highlight with Titanium White. Soften all shadows and outlines.

19. Paint the lips with the no. 1 round using a mixture of Mix 1 + Alizarin Crimson + Burnt Umber.

NECK AND HAIR

20. Using a no. 4 flat, paint the area of flesh under the beard with Mix 1 and darken with Burnt Umber.

21. Paint the hair on the head, mustache and chin with Mix 5 on a no. 4 flat. Lighten with Titanium White on a ¹/₂-inch (13mm) whisk and blend in the direction the hair grows.

22. With the no. 1 round brush and the no. 6/0 liner, add lines of Titanium White thinned with paint thinner to an ink-like consistency.

COAT, COLLAR AND CUFF

23. Basecoat the coat using the no. 6 flat brush and Cadmium Red Light. Darken with Alizarin Crimson. Darken further with Burnt Umber. Use a slip-slap brushstroke to blend, but don't overblend.

24. Paint the darkest areas of the collar and cuff with Mix 5 on a no. 6 flat. Paint the light areas with Titanium White. Blend these colors together with a whisk brush, following the lie of the fur. To allow the paint to move more easily, dampen the brush slightly in paint thinner and dab on a paper towel. Then add tints of Mix 4 to the dark areas.

25. Use a no. 1 round and a no. 6/0 liner to add lines of Titanium White thinned with paint thinner.

GOBLET

26. Basecoat the goblet with Yellow Ochre using a no. 2 flat brush. Darken the shadowed side with Burnt Umber and with Ivory Black. Add tints of Cadmium Red Light.

27. Paint the vertical design with Burnt Umber and with Ivory Black. Highlight these areas with Cadmium Yellow Light and with Titanium White. Use a no. 2 flat.

28. Still using the no. 2 flat add the horizontal bands and the dots with Cadmium Yellow Light and with Titanium White. Paint shadows of the bands and dots with Burnt Umber.

HAND

29. Using a no. 4 flat, basecoat the dark flesh areas with Mix 1 and the light flesh areas with Mix 2. Blend only slightly.

30. Add shadows with Mix 1 + Burnt Umber. Paint highlights with Titanium White. Blend slightly.

HOLLY

31. Make sure the hair and forehead are dry and then transfer the pattern of the holly and holly shadows.

32. Basecoat the leaves with Mix 3 on a no. 4 flat. Add shading with Ivory Black. Add highlighting with Titanium White and with Cadmium Yellow Light.

33. Paint the veins and leaf outlining with a no. 1 round brush and Mix 4. Add highlights with Titanium White.

34. Paint the berries with a no. 1 round and Cadmium Red Light. Shade with Alizarin Crimson.

35. Paint the holly-leaf shadows on Sir Christmas' forehead with Mix 1 and Burnt Umber on a no. 4 flat.

COMPLETED
SIR CHRISTMAS STOCKING

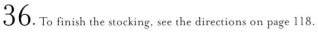

36. To finish the stocking, see the directions on page 118.

RESOURCES

BRUSHES

Bette Byrd Brushes
P.O. Box 2526
Duluth, GA 30136
Phone: 770-623-6097

PAINTS AND MEDIUMS

ColArt Americas
  (Winsor & Newton)
11 Constitution Avenue
Piscataway, NJ 08855-1396
Phone: 732-562-0770
www.winsornewton.com

Plaid Enterprises, Inc. (FolkArt)
P.O. Box 7600
Norcross, GA 30091-7600
Phone: 678-291-8100
www.plaidonline.com

SURFACES

Viking Woodcrafts
1317 8th Street S.E.
Waseca, MN 56093
Phone: 1-800-328-0116

GENERAL SUPPLIES

Masterson Art Products, Inc.
  (for Sta-Wet Palette)
P.O. Box 10775
Glendale, AZ 85318
Phone: 1-800-965-2675
www.mastersonart.com

3M Scotch
  (for Plastic Tape 471 Blue)
Phone: 1-888-3M HELPS
www.3m.com

Pat Wakefield
  (for Old World Santa pant packets)
P.O. Box 3245
Shawnee Mission, KS 66203
Phone: 913-649-8318
E-mail: pat@patwakefield.com
www.patwakefield.com.

CANADIAN RETAILERS

Crafts Canada
2745 29th St. N.E.
Calgary, AL, T1Y 7B5

Folk Art Enterprises
P.O. Box 1088
Ridgetown, ON, N0P 2C0
Tel: 888-214-0062

MacPherson Craft Wholesale
83 Queen St. E.
P.O. Box 1870
St. Mary's, ON, N4X 1C2
Tel: 519-284-1741

Maureen McNaughton Enterprises Inc.
RR #2
Belwood, ON, N0B 1J0
Tel: 519-843-5648
Fax: 519-843-6022
E-mail:
    maureen.mcnaughton.ent.inc
    @sympatico.ca
www.maureenmcnaughton.com

Mercury Art & Craft Supershop
332 Wellington St.
London, ON, N6C 4P7
Tel: 519-434-1636

Town & Country Folk Art Supplies
93 Green Lane
Thornhill, ON, L3T 6K6
Tel: 905-882-0199

U.K. RETAILERS

Art Express
Design House
Sizers Court
Yeadon LS9 6DP
Tel: 0800 731 4185
www.artexpress.co.uk

Atlantis Art Materials
146 Brick Lane
London E1 6RU
Tel: 020 7377 8855

Crafts World (head office)
No. 8 North Street, Guildford
Surrey GU1 4AF
Tel: 07000 757070

Green & Stone
259 King's Road
London SW3 5EL
Tel: 020 7352 0837
E-mail:
  greenandstone@enterprise.net

Hobby Crafts (head office)
River Court
Southern Sector
Bournemouth International Airport
Christchurch
Dorset BH23 6SE
Tel: 0800 272387

Homecrafts Direct
P.O. Box 38
Leicester LE1 9BU
Tel: 0116 251 3139

INDEX

The Best in Decorative Painting Instruction and Inspiration is from *North Light Books!*

ISBN 1-58180-105-X,
paperback, 128 pages,
#31794-K

Learn to paint your favorite Christmas themes, including Santas, angels, elves and more, on everything from glittering ornaments to festive albums. Renowned decorative painter John Gutcher shows you how with 9 all-new, step-by-step projects. He makes mastering tricky details simple with special tips for painting fur, hair, richly textured clothing and realistic flesh tones.

ISBN 1-58180-364-8,
paperback, 128 pages,
#32378-K

Paint your own one-of-a-kind, heirloom-quality ornaments, tableware and gift items—and make this Christmas one to remember! Carol Mays provides 16 fun, heartwarming projects. Each one includes detailed patterns, step-by-step instructions and full color photos that ensure success. There's a variety of cheerful designs to choose from, including Santa Claus, snowmen, gingerbread kids, strokework flowers, winter scenes, decorative borders and more.

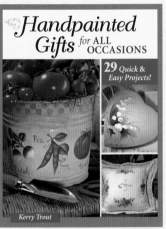

ISBN 1-58180-426-1,
paperback, 144 pages,
#32590-K

Kerry Trout helps you create fabulous gifts without difficult painting techniques to master. Inside Handpainted Gifts for all Occasions you'll discover 29 easy-to-paint projects for holidays, family events and seasonal displays. Included are 12 "Quick Projects" that can be painted in an afternoon or less with inexpensive surfaces that are available at any craft or discount store. Each project features straightforward instruction, a materials list, color swatch chart, and traceable patterns as well as colorful photos of the finished project.

ISBN 1-58180-261-7,
paperback, 144 pages,
#32126-K

Learn how to enhance your paintings with the classic elegance of decorative gold, silver and variegated accents. Rebecca Baer illustrates detailed gilding techniques with step-by-step photos and invaluable problem-solving advice. Perfect for your home or gift giving, there are 13 exciting projects in all, each one enhanced with lustrous leafing effects.

These books and other fine North Light titles are available from your local art & craft retailer, bookstore, online supplier or by calling 1-800-448-0915.